A MAN AS PRIEST

IN HIS HOME

Samuel E. Waldron, Ph.D.

with

Benjamin Hoak

RBAP
Owensboro, KY

Scripture taken from the NEW AMERICAN STANDARD BIBLE®, Copyright®
1960, 1962, 1963, 1968, 1971, 1972, 1973, 1975, 1977, 1995 by The Lockman
Foundation.
Used by permission.

Requests for information should be sent to:

RBAP
349 Sunrise Terrace
Palmdale, CA 93551
rb@rbap.net
www.rbap.net

Printed in the United States of America.

Cover design by Kalós Grafx Studios | www.kalosgrafx.com

ISBN-13: 978-0-9802179-7-1

TABLE OF CONTENTS

CHAPTER ONE

PRIESTLY MINISTRY

Christians are called to many things as we follow God and his holy Word, but two duties stand out. When asked the greatest responsibility his followers should have, Christ didn't hesitate before asserting that love and service to God come first, above all else. With all of our heart, soul, mind and strength, we are to love the God who created and redeemed us. Our second greatest responsibility focuses on the people who make up the fabric of our lives. Christ calls us to love our neighbors – i.e., whoever may cross our path – as ourselves. That's a tall order to fill given our tremendous capacity to seek our own interests.

Love for our neighbors involves more than just fuzzy feelings for the family who lives next door. Often, the best way we can show love is to meet people's needs by serving them or ministering to them. Paul emphasizes this when he tells the Galatians that Christ set them free so that they might "through love serve one another" (Galatians 5:13).

The concern in this book is rooted in that great calling to serve one another. As Christian husbands and fathers, how should we view our ministry to our family? When our teenager has just vaulted into the annals of history with the stupidity and sinfulness of his behavior, how should we respond? When we let our wives down, how do we respond? When our families are struggling, how do we help them? What kind of ministry should we have in our home?

Priestly Ministry

To support the ultimate conclusion of this book that a man serves as a priest in his home, we must begin with the idea that *all* Christian ministry is priestly in character. When we talk about ministry, we're referring not just to the official duties of pastors, but to the whole spectrum of dealings among Christians, including such things as counseling, teaching, praying, rebuking, encouraging, helping, etc. To prove the idea that all Christian ministry is priestly in character, we'll look at four arguments.

The Presupposition

A presupposition is to an argument what a foundation is to a house. As the children's song says, "The wise man built his house upon the rock/the foolish man built his house upon the sand." Just as the rock is the foundation of the wise man's house, so a good presupposition is the foundation of any well-constructed argument.

The presupposition of the argument that all Christian ministry is priestly in character is simply that the primary office of Christ is his *priestly* office. According to Scripture, Christ exercises the offices of prophet, priest and king. He is the prophet like unto Moses, the priest according to the order of Melchizedek and the kingly son of David. Each individual office is essential to who Christ is and what he came to do, but his priestly office is the most basic.

This is true, first of all, because of Christ's saving purpose. "For God did not send His Son into the world to judge the world, but that the world might be saved through Him" (John 3:17). In order to judge the world, it would have been sufficient for Christ to be a prophet (to tell us what we ought to have done) and a king (to condemn us for not having done it). But to save the world, he had to serve as a priest (to offer a sacrifice in our place). Matthew 20:28 says, "... the Son of Man did not come to be served, but to serve, and to give His life a ransom for many." Christ's sacrifice – his essential work and the ultimate reason he came to earth – was the work of a priest.

Christ's priestly work also shines through in his necessary incarnation. Hebrews 2:17 says, "Therefore, He had to be made like His brethren in all things, so that He might become a merciful and faithful high priest ..." An angel might have been a prophet, and God is our King, but a man had to be a priest for the human race, for only a man could offer the necessary sacrifice on behalf of his fellow men.

Further, we see evidence of Christ's priesthood in his peculiar presence in the church. Revelation 1:13 says, "And in the middle of the lampstands I saw one like a son of man, clothed in a robe reaching to the feet, and girded across his chest with a golden sash." This glorious vision of Christ's majesty presents him as a priest; the seven golden lampstands are his churches – reminiscent of the temple – where the exalted Lord walks in garments like those of a priest.

The Proof

We know from the Scriptures that all Christian ministry must take place in the name of Christ and as a part of the body of Christ. Colossians 3:17 tells us, "Whatever you do in word or deed, do all in the name of the Lord Jesus." Romans 12:4-8 and 1 Corinthians 12:13 make it clear that the church is the body of Christ, and it is as part of this body that we are given gifts to minister to one another. When we reach others in ministry, we do so only through our risen Christ as a priest, and according to his law. As Galatians 6:1-2 says, "… restore such a one in a spirit of gentleness … and thereby fulfill the law of Christ."

Elsewhere, the Bible calls the body of Christ a royal priesthood (1 Peter 2:5, 9; Revelation 1:6), and as such, its ministry must conform to its identity. When the church ministers to men and women in a God-glorifying manner, it retains its identity as a holy priesthood. When the church focuses on what pleases men rather than on what is an acceptable sacrifice to God, it loses that God-given identity.

Because Christian ministry represents Christ, whose fundamental office is that of priest, the ultimate goal of our service as Christians must be *redemptive*, just as a priest's role is redemptive. The Bible is full of priests because the overarching theme of the Bible is the redemption of sinners. From creation, to Adam's fall, to the Old Testament covenants, to Christ's death on the cross and the beginning of the church, the whole of Scripture focuses on redemption. As 1 Peter 3:18 says, "For Christ also died for sins once for all, the just for the unjust, in order that He might bring us to God." Every part of our priestly ministry to others must take this context of redemption into account, for without the redemption of our great High Priest, we would all likewise perish.

The Prejudice

Many Christians will see no problem with the idea of acting in a priestly and redemptive manner toward sinners, but some may have a prejudice against it. Such prejudice represents a tendency to react to the spirit of our day with so much force that we swing to the opposite extreme.

This has been the age of cultural leniency and liberalism, where no one is accountable for anything – especially their own actions – and everyone is considered a victim. In our day, we have seen the philosophical denial of sin and the promotion of self-esteem as the most important human value and character quality. Drunkenness, addiction and sexual deviancy are no longer sins – they are illnesses or genetic problems, and sometimes not even that. Perhaps the only sin left is to take away someone's self-esteem. Our age has been a time of evangelical easy-believism, antinomianism and loose churchmanship. The law of God has been widely jettisoned, and living in sin doesn't seem to contradict the essence of what it means to be a Christian and church member.

In many quarters, a backlash has set in against this perspective, making this also an era where anyone can express an opinion, no matter how outrageous. Many commentators rail without mercy against rampant leniency and liberalism, but as Christians, we must beware of reacting so harshly to sin and lack of responsibility that we forget the compassion that Christ showed to sinners. We must react with kindness in the midst of our righteous anger. We must remember that we were once children of wrath as well, and Christ graciously saved us according to his sovereign will. We must treat others as Christ, our priestly example, would.

The Practice

The heart of how we minister practically is contained in Hebrews 4:14-5:3; a passage that dwells on what it means to be a priest:

> Therefore, since we have a great high priest who has passed through the heavens, Jesus the Son of God, let us hold fast our confession. For we do not have a high priest who cannot sympathize with our weaknesses, but One who has been tempted in all things as we are, yet without sin. Therefore let us draw near with confidence to the throne of grace, so that we may receive mercy and find grace to help in time of need. For every high priest taken from among men is appointed on behalf of men in things pertaining to God, in order to offer both gifts and sacrifices for sins; he can deal gently with the ignorant and misguided, since he himself also is beset with weakness; and because of it he is obligated to offer sacrifices for sins, as for the people, so also for himself.

There is one qualification to bear in mind in the using of this passage: Our ministry should be on the basis of Christ's once-for-all sacrifice for sins as a priestly mediator. *We are not to repeat the sacrifice of our High Priest, but we are to embody his spirit.* With that in mind, we'll consider five aspects of priestly ministry, based on the passage above.

Five Aspects of Priestly Ministry

Let's consider five aspects of priestly ministry from Hebrews 4:14-5:3.

The Goal of Priestly Ministry: "appointed on behalf of men"

If God were not concerned about the well-being of men, he would not have created the office of priest. The goal of priestly ministry is to do good to the souls of men. That is to say, priests exist for the sake of men. All ministry must be God-centered, but it must also be man-purposed.

The Focus of Priestly Ministry: "in things pertaining to God"

The focus of priestly ministry is reconciling men to God by correcting their standing before him. The relationship of a person's never-dying soul with the eternal God is a foundational concern that should rise above physical or emotional well-being. This concern supersedes interpersonal relationships and focuses on an individual's vertical relationship with God. When we approach someone such as a fellow church member with the intention of engaging in Christian ministry, the primary question in our hearts should be, "What is this person's relationship to God, and what can I do to improve it?" If he is an unbeliever, we should aim to lead him to a saving knowledge of Christ. If she already knows Christ, we should seek to strengthen her relationship to him.

The Concern of Priestly Ministry: "for sins"

The chief concern of priestly ministry is to deal with the sin that has ruined someone's relationship with God. In the case of our Savior, this involved a once-for-all sacrifice for sin. In our case, we must simply try to help people see their sin and repent so that it may be covered by the blood of Christ. Sin – not emotional or psychological problems – is the key issue for a priest. As long as any supposed ministry leaves sin untouched, it falls short of being truly priestly. This doesn't mean that Christian ministry cannot legitimately address physical or emotional needs. But, where sin is the problem (or at least part of the problem) true Christian ministry must eventually address that sin.

The Spirit of Priestly Ministry: "he can deal gently"

This is the only place this Greek word for "gently" occurs in the New Testament. It is composed of two root words – one is the common Greek word for *emotion* or *feeling*, from which we get our words *pathos*, *passion* and *compassion*. The other root word is the common Greek word for *measure*, from which we derive our English word *meter*. This word conveys the idea of moderation or self-restraint. So, to deal gently literally means to deal with *measured passion*. The Greek dictionary says the word means to exercise moderation toward someone in emotions and passions.

When a friend commits a deep offense against us, our tendency is to be angry. (This isn't always wrong – certain offenses should provoke righteous anger.) Even though we want to be angry, we still must deal gently with our friend. When our children have behaved badly, our tendency as parents is to become angry, embarrassed, ashamed, disappointed – these are all emotional reactions. As priests, we must measure our emotional responses so they don't come pouring forth in an overwhelming deluge.

Strength is found in gentleness because ruling over our emotions requires the exercise of self-control and wisdom. Repentance is never easy, but we shouldn't add our own sinful anger as an additional obstacle to a sinner's reconciliation to God. If someone has sinned, our duty is to approach them in the way most likely to help rather than hinder their repentance. We must never allow ourselves to become the issue – our goal is not to satisfy ourselves. Instead, we want to act as mediators to resolve the true issue of the sin separating God and the sinner. This was Job's burden when he offered sacrifices on behalf of his children, as Job 1:5 records, "Perhaps my sons have sinned and cursed God in their heart." Job is concerned not with himself, but with his children's relationship with God.

The Perspective of Priestly Ministry: "with the ignorant and misguided"

The Bible presents many potential ways to treat sin, but not all are priestly. Sinners are not enemies to be attacked, defended against or fled from. They're not unclean people to be avoided or good people who merely made a mistake. Their self-esteem won't suffer in the face of exhortation. A priest should simply treat sinners as ignorant, misguided people who need to be instructed and led back to the correct way, as the text in Hebrews reminds us.

How do we look at sinners to whom we must minister? Is our tendency to avoid them, or do we have a redemptive and priestly perspective that seeks to engage them? If we approach them in a spirit of humility, as sinners redeemed by grace, gently and carefully guiding them through God's redemptive Word, then we are acting as true priests.

Application

To apply what it means to practice a priestly approach to Christian ministry, imagine a teenager and his father. It's late at night, and the father is about to walk into his son's bedroom to continue dealing with an argument from earlier in the evening. It began with the father discovering his son's sin and continued with the disgraced son defending himself against his angry, disappointed and embarrassed dad. They exchanged angry words, and the conversation continued downhill from there. As the dad prepares to resume the discussion, he reminds himself that he isn't trying judge his son, but to point him to God. His son's sin against God is the issue, not his own disappointment.

He knocks softly, waits for a murmured response and slowly pushes open the door. Neither the father nor the son knows exactly what to say in the momentary silence, but the father begins by confessing his own sin of anger in the original conversation. Silently asking for grace to keep him from losing his temper all over again, he attempts to point out the sin his son committed against God. He patiently answers one objection after another, and he gently instructs his son from the Word of God.

In this conversation, the father acknowledges his own problems repeatedly so his son can find no excuse in his father for his sin. The father confesses that he has set a bad example many times and that he should have taken advantage of more opportunities to teach his son. As he does this, he is crucifying his innate desire to defend himself and attack his son.

The discussion ends not just with the words, "You're grounded," but with a call to repentance and a plea that the teenager will make things right with God. The father prayerfully waits, hopeful that his son will confess his sin and pray for cleansing in the blood of the great High Priest. This is authentic priestly Christian ministry.

If we are struggling deeply with a sense of how unclean, weak, and sinful we are, or if we're overwhelmed with things we can scarcely forgive ourselves for, we have hope. Christ will always receive us – he is our great High Priest who is gentle, who won't avoid or reject anyone, who is concerned about how to restore our relationship with God. He is a Savior whose very essence and identity flows from our salvation. Nothing should stop us from running into the arms of such a Savior as this!

CHAPTER TWO

THE SCRIPTURAL WARRANT

The idea that a man is a priest in his home follows naturally from the thesis that all Christian ministry is priestly in character. Nevertheless, this subject confronts men with some of the most difficult responsibilities we will ever face. When we realize our duty and feel our sin and weakness in this area, we must constantly remind ourselves of the grace and promises God has given to us. We cannot make progress in our own strength. We will only grow up and into our responsibilities with God's help.

As we begin this growth process, we'll look at the scriptural warrant for the man as a priest in his home. In subsequent chapters, we'll examine a classic portrait of such a man and then study his special roles and spiritual qualifications. Three main arguments – moving from general to specific – will provide us with an outline for a biblical apologetic for a man as a priest in his home.

Spiritual Leadership

First, priests in Israel exercised many functions of spiritual leadership identical to duties that a man must exercise in his home. Ephesians 6:4, the classical biblical statement of what a man should be as a father, says men must practice spiritual leadership in the home: "And, fathers, do not provoke your children to anger; but bring them up in the discipline and instruction of the Lord."

In this verse, the man is addressed (*"And, fathers"*), the home is concerned (*"your children"*) and the spirit is priestly (*"do not provoke your children to anger"*). Fathers are to be gentle, wise and benevolent in their leadership, and we have already seen that priests are to be gentle and gracious in their ministries. The passage also implies the spiritual nature of the work of fathers. Just as Paul tells children in Ephesians 6:1 that they should obey their parents "in the

Lord," the same phrase in verse four underscores that the discipline and instruction in view have a spiritual focus.

Such spiritual leadership involves performing in the home many of the functions priests carried out in Israel. Later chapters will expand on these purposes. For now, it's enough to note that the five special roles of the priests of Israel line up nicely with the roles a man should play in his home. The priests in Israel were intercessors in prayer (2 Chronicles 30:27), communicators of blessing (Numbers 6:22-27), directors of worship (1 Kings 4:2), instructors in Scripture (Malachi 2:7) and judges in holy things (Deuteronomy 17:9, 12). A man must be each of these things for his family if he is to provide true spiritual leadership in his home. Such parallels strongly suggest that men are indeed spiritual priests in their home.

Early History

Second, priests in the Old Testament were viewed as spiritual fathers, so it is natural to think of fathers today as spiritual priests. Two interesting biblical facts lend credence to this argument: the original order after creation and the common thinking in Israel.

The Old Testament's history of the period prior to the Mosaic covenant and the establishment of the Levitical priesthood makes evident that fathers naturally functioned as priests in their homes. Even setting aside the special priesthoods of Melchizedek and Jethro (who served as priests of cities or tribes), Noah, Abraham, Isaac, Jacob and Job all seemed to have acted as priests for their families by offering sacrifices and burnt offerings according to God's original order.

The general attitude in Israel also points us in this direction, as the two following verses show. Judges 17:10 reads, "Micah then said to him, 'Dwell with me and be a father and a priest to me, and I will give you ten pieces of silver a year, a suit of clothes, and your maintenance.'" Further, Judges 18:19 says, "And they said to him, 'Be silent, put your hand over your mouth and come with us, and be to us a father and a priest. Is it better for you to be a priest to the house of one man, or to be priest to a tribe and family in Judah?'"

These passages occur in the last five chapters of Judges – a section that underscores the highly chaotic condition of Israel during the period when judges ruled.

The point of interest in these verses is that during the nation's early history, the Israelites' widespread thinking closely associated the roles of father and priest. Micah (an Ephraimite) and members of the tribe of Dan use the phrase "a father and a priest" while speaking to a Levite who had sojourned in Judah. With four of the twelve tribes represented in the transaction, the link between father and priest seems to have been common to at least a third of the people of Israel. When combined with the period before the Mosaic covenant, this thinking shows that the association of fatherhood and priesthood was not an aberration unique to this period of the Judges, but a common inheritance from the patriarchs of Israel.

The Model of Christ

The third argument provides an even more compelling reason that men must be priests in their homes. Precisely at the point of his priestly work, Christ is held up as the great model of the highest duty of husbands to their wives. As Ephesians 5:25-27 explains:

> Husbands, love your wives, just as Christ also loved the church and gave Himself up for her; that He might sanctify her, having cleansed her by the washing of water with the word, that He might present to Himself the church in all her glory, having no spot or wrinkle or any such thing; but that she should be holy and blameless.

Since husbands are commanded here to love their wives in the same manner that Christ loved the church, it follows logically that if Christ's work is priestly, a husband would in some sense be a priest to his wife. Even a quick glance at the verses makes evident the priestly nature of Christ's actions, drawing a clear line to the husband's role as priest. Four specific words have clear connections to the priesthood.

In verse 25, the verb phrase *gave himself up* speaks of a priestly action. The closest contextual usage of the verb is Ephesians 5:2, which says, "and walk in love, just as Christ also loved you and *gave Himself up* for us, an offering and a sacrifice to God as a fragrant aroma." Here, the phrase speaks of Christ as a priest who gives himself in love as an offering to God.

The word *sanctify* in Ephesians 5:26 also specifies a priestly activity. Several passages in Hebrews use this meaning of *sanctify*, including Hebrews 2:11; 10:10; 10:14 and 13:12. With this sanctification, a priest makes people fit to enter the holy precincts of worship where God's holy presence abides. This use of *sanctify* is distinctive compared to most other uses in the New Testament, where the word refers to the Holy Spirit making God's people more holy.

The third phrase with priestly connotations – *having cleansed* – is also found in Ephesians 5:26. Again, the book of Hebrews is relevant. Hebrews 9:13-14 says:

> For if the blood of goats and bulls and the ashes of a heifer sprinkling those who have been defiled, sanctify for the cleansing of the flesh, how much more will the blood of Christ, who through the eternal Spirit offered Himself without blemish to God, cleanse your conscience from dead works to serve the living God?

This is the only place in the entire New Testament other than Ephesians 5:26 where the verbs *sanctify* and *cleanse* are used together. Christ, "as a high priest of the good things to come" (Hebrews 9:11), sanctifies and cleanses his people by his blood, making them fit for the presence of a holy God and removing from their consciences the sense of moral defilement created by their sins. Fourth, the word *washing* in Ephesians 5:26 is also closely associated with the activity of a priest. Hebrews 9:13 and 10:21-22 describe priests who used water mixed with the ashes of a red heifer to cleanse ceremonial defilement, as the Old Covenant directed in Numbers 19:9, 17. Paul points to that priestly activity in Ephesians 5:26, when he speaks of the "washing of water with the word."

This priestly language makes clear that Paul is indeed thinking of Christ as a priest when he presents him in Ephesians 5:25-27 as an example of what a husband should be. A man must imitate Christ's priestly behavior if he would be a priest to his wife and in his home.

Since solid scriptural warrant exists to assert that a man should act as a priest in his home, we must examine ourselves in that light. Just as an ultraviolet lamp can reveal realities previously unseen to the naked eye, we often discover new aspects of our Christian lives by the light of Scripture. As the heads of our homes, we have often seen ourselves as husbands and fathers, and perhaps even as prophets or kings. But have we ever seen ourselves as priests? Under the intense brightness of God's word, we should take notice of our priestly garments and begin to live up to the duties that a priest must accomplish.

Application

We can draw several lessons from these considerations.

Loving Our Wives

First, we learn something of what it means for us to be a priest to our wife. We must love her by showing an abiding concern for her spiritual welfare and progress, and we must seek that welfare by washing her with the priestly, cleansing water of the Word. We should also speak to our wife regarding these spiritual matters. We can't teach her if we don't speak to her. But these two things – loving and speaking – are just the areas where so many men fail. We must confess our sin to God, our wife, and ourselves, and begin by the grace of God to treat our wife in a priestly manner.

When a Man Fails as a Priest

Wives and children should also respect a man's priestly authority and support him in his priestly roles, even when he fails in them. Hannah is a wonderful example of this in 1Samuel 1. Eli was far from an ideal priest, and Hannah must have known that. Despite this truth, she responds respectfully to his false accusation of drunkenness with a simple, "No, my lord" in 1 Samuel 1:15. Hannah's example should encourage us to ask our wives and children to support us and submit to us even though our best efforts often fall short. When a wife uses her husband's remaining sin as an excuse for her lack of respect, she needs to be reminded that there was only one perfect man who ever lived – and she isn't married to him! Kids should remember that no matter how much they want to be like their father, he's not perfect. Our wife and children may think we have no right to question and exhort them because of our failures and sins. It is true that we must humbly confess those sins. But, even a flawed priest must fulfill his duties. We will sometimes make mistakes, just as our wife and children will. Given our sinful natures, the only way for us not to make such mistakes would be to abandon our role completely, but that would make for even worse problems. It may be difficult to give respect to a sinful man, but those who don't give him that respect will regret it in the end.

Preparation for Priesthood

Even a man who is not yet a husband or father should see his need for priestly qualifications if he ever wants to be a proper husband and father in the future. If we desire to become the leader of a home, we must possess the ability to fulfill all the necessary roles of a priest. We must be concerned about God's holiness and people's sinfulness. We must have the spirit of a priest at least in some measure. A priest exists for the sake of others. So, peculiar self-denial is a requirement for priesthood. If a young man is so self-indulgent that he can't control his money, time, emotions and desires now, that's probably a good sign he's not yet qualified to serve as a priest in his family's home. If he's so irresponsible that he isn't leading a productive life now, a prospective wife will not look at him as a man she wants to lead her. We must prepare now for future responsibilities.

A Priest's Hope

Finally, we are reminded of the most fundamental office and work of Christ. It is crucial that we always keep the basic and central character of Christ's priesthood in view. The Medieval church largely lost its vision of Christ as a compassionate high priest and looked at him more and more as an austere, exalted king. Weary souls turned to Mary and the saints to act as their mediators with this distant king. To avoid this trap, we must remind ourselves of our basic problem. We need a priest to minister to us because in ourselves we are condemned, defiled and excluded from God's presence. We must be cleansed, justified and sanctified by Christ our high priest if we are to have any glimpse of God's presence.

Christ is our only hope. The moral disgust we stir in God's heart is placated solely by the sacrifice of Christ. His priestly washing is the only way to cleanse the moral defilement that precludes us from being in God's presence. This great cleansing is possible because Christ is our burnt offering; consumed and burned up in our place by the fire of God's wrath. Out of the ashes of that ultimate burnt offering is made the only water that can cleanse us from our impurities. All men everywhere should believe in Christ and go to him as their priest. Only the man who realizes his own desperate need of a priest – and trusts Christ to fulfill that need can truly serve as a priest in his home.

CHAPTER THREE
THE CLASSIC PORTRAIT

To better understand the concept of a man as a priest in his home, it will help to take a look at the classic scriptural portrait of such a man. We've just been through several logical arguments, but humans are much more than merely logical beings. Logic is often not enough to convince people of an idea. Warm, living examples are a crucial component of moving men and women to a true view of their duty. Perhaps this is why much of the Bible comes to us in historical narratives rather than in doctrinal treatises.

We're going to examine the life of Job, a unique figure in Scripture and a prime example of a man who was truly a priest in his home. The classic portrait of his priesthood is found in Job 1:1-5:

> There was a man in the land of Uz whose name was Job; and that man was blameless, upright, fearing God and turning away from evil. Seven sons and three daughters were born to him. His possessions also were 7,000 sheep, 3,000 camels, 500 yoke of oxen, 500 female donkeys, and very many servants; and that man was the greatest of all the men of the east. His sons used to go and hold a feast in the house of each one on his day, and they would send and invite their three sisters to eat and drink with them. When the days of feasting had completed their cycle, Job would send and consecrate them, rising up early in the morning and offering burnt offerings according to the number of them all; for Job said, "Perhaps my sons have sinned and cursed God in their hearts." Thus Job did continually.

The Certainty of Job's Priesthood

The first thing we must realize is that Job was certainly acting as a priest to his family – verse five says he consecrated (literally, *sanctified*) his children and offered burnt offerings for them. Two

phrases in particular stand out: *Job would send and consecrate them*
and *offering burnt offerings*. The most enlightening parallel passage
to the first phrase is probably Exodus 19:7-15, where God requires
Moses to "go to the people and consecrate them today and
tomorrow, and let them wash their garments; and let them be ready
for the third day, for on the third day the LORD will come down on
Mount Sinai in the sight of all the people." Applying this passage to
Job, we can conclude that by this ritual and spiritual cleansing, Job's
sons and daughters were preparing themselves for the holy worship
of God. Job's sending and sanctifying his children implies they were
required to attend the worship Job led. Even though some were adult
children, Job brought all the holy pressure he could to bear on them
as he assumed his right to lead them in the worship of God.

Job was also literally offering offerings for his children. The
Hebrew root word for offer speaks of making something go up. The
idea is that the smoke of the burning sacrifice would ascend to God
and soothe his nostrils from the stench of sin committed by those
whom the sacrifice represented. The burnt offering was also a sin
offering – a pointed symbol of the way God forgives sin through
substitutionary suffering. Hebrews 5:1 and 8:3-4 point out that one
of the distinctives of a priest is that he offers sacrifices. So, in
making burnt offerings for his children, Job was clearly acting as a
priest.

The Circumstances of Job's Priesthood

Job's physical surroundings – his history, family, finances, social
situation and morals – offer more clues regarding his priesthood.

Job's History

Historically, Job's identity is something of a mystery, although there
are a few hints scattered throughout the Old Testament. In Job 1:3,
he is described as "the greatest of all the men of the East." A
comparison of this phrase with 1 Kings 4:30 ("Solomon's wisdom
surpassed the wisdom of all the sons of the east and all the wisdom

of Egypt") and Genesis 29:1 ("Then Jacob went on his journey, and came to the land of the sons of the east") leads to the conclusion that he did not live in the Promised Land, and was not a Jew or one of the promised seed of Jacob. The name Uz (Job lived in the land of Uz – Job 1:1) occurs seven other places in the Bible, but it is likely that the Uz mentioned in the book of Job refers to the son of Aram described in Genesis 10:23. If so, the city of Uz was located to the northeast of modern-day Palestine in the vicinity of Syria.

Another clue surfaces in Job 42:16: "And after this, Job lived 140 years, and saw his sons, and his grandsons, four generations." Since he had ten children and had built a considerable reputation prior to his trials, and he lived 140 years after them, he must have been close to 200 years old when he died. This makes his life span greater than that of Abraham, who lived to be 175 years old (Genesis 25:7), which was considered a ripe old age. Life spans decreased rapidly after the flood, so this places Job at or even before the time of Abraham. He also fits well in this time period because there is no mention of Abraham, Israel, Moses or any of the distinctives of the Abrahamic Covenant in the entire book of Job. His world apparently knew nothing of God's special promise to Abraham's offspring. So, Job must have lived before that covenant was established.

Additionally, the exercise of Job's family priesthood places him in a time preceding the Mosaic period. When the Mosaic Covenant took effect, the priesthood was restricted by law to the tribe of Levi and the sons of Aaron. Prior to that, though, we have records of many legitimate priesthoods that were exercised by others. Melchizedek is called the priest of the Most High God in Genesis 14. Jethro is sympathetically recognized as the priest of Midian in Exodus 18. More significantly, Noah, Abraham and Jacob all appear to have exercised priesthoods similar to Job's in their own families (Genesis 8:20-22; 22:9-13; 35:1-7).

Job's Family

Job 1:2 makes plain the fact that Job was the head of a large family, with at least ten children, a wife and many servants. Verses four and five make it clear that Job engaged in priestly activity by offering sacrifices in behalf of his children. It is not as a priest of his nation or tribe that Job is presented here, but as a priest in his home.

Job's Finances

Financially, Job was a wealthy man, as the lengthy description of his possessions in verse three shows. This description provides the basis for us to understand the devastating losses Job later suffers, but it also conveys that Job must have been a very busy man with such a vast personal and business empire to administer.

Job's Social Situation

Job's social circumstances were also enviable. Partly because of his wealth and partly because of his moral character, Job was regarded as the greatest of the sons of the east. He was of high and responsible standing in society and in his nation, sitting in the gates of his own city and the capital city as he held court. In the Old Testament, Moses (the mediator of the Old Covenant), David (the king of Israel), and Mordecai (the prime minister for the king of Persia), among others, are all described as great. The same word is used here to describe Job, based on the amount of influence and social stature he possesses.

Job's Morals

In the realm of morals, Job was an admirable man as well. Job 1:1 provides us with a description of his moral character. He is blameless, upright, fearing God and turning away from evil. This does not mean, of course, that Job was sinless. Job himself confesses his sin in Job 42:6, when he says, "Therefore I retract and I repent in dust and ashes."

But while we shouldn't hold Job's uprightness up as sinless perfection, neither should we underestimate his excellent moral character. His character is critical for the entire message of the book of Job. The overriding question of the book of Job is "why do the righteous suffer?" For this question to make sense, we must know at the outset that Job was a genuinely and consistently righteous man. We should not view Job's actions as the desecration of the priestly office by a wicked man, but rather as the exemplary activities of a righteous man who possesses outstanding moral character.

The Character of Job's Priesthood

Job 1:4-5 offers several perspectives on the character of Job's priesthood. The context of his priestly activity was the cycle of feasts described in verse four – most likely birthday celebrations, if "on his day" signifies each son's birthday. Job's use of this identical phrase to describe his own birthday in Job 3:1 particularly supports this interpretation. The idea is that each son would invite his brothers and sisters to a banquet celebrating his birthday.

Verse five says that Job's offering consistently took place when "the days of feasting had completed their cycle." His children's birthday celebrations apparently lasted several days, so Job would rise early to offer his burnt offerings the morning after each celebration ended. Assuming the birthday interpretation is correct, he would do this at least seven times every year. Such a periodic sacrifice is a remarkable evidence of Job's consistent family godliness.

The priority of Job's priesthood in his life is epitomized in one phrase in verse five: "rising up early in the morning." Generally speaking, the things that make us get out of bed early in the morning are of high priority to us. These sacrifices had this kind of priority for Job. His business responsibilities took so much of his time that he had to rise early in the morning to make sure he accomplished his spiritual duties before the pressures of the day crowded in.

Job 1:5 also tells us of the spiritual motive which prompted Job to make these periodic offerings: "for Job said, 'Perhaps my sons have sinned and cursed God in their hearts.'" Job's statement tells us that his sacrifices were far more than empty, external, legalistic rituals. They were a heartfelt use of the appointed form of Old Testament worship, with a view to delivering his children from the anger of an offended God. Job was determined that as far as any human being could do so, he would lead his children to the mercy seat of God so they might experience His grace. Because of this burden – one that can only be understood by parents of unsaved children – Job used all the moral authority he could bring to bear on them.

Job's priesthood was also marked by its perseverance. Verse five ends with the statement, "Thus Job did continually" (literally, *all the days)*. Job was marked by great consistency in this and the other associated manifestations of his family godliness. He offered these sacrifices like clockwork after each of his children's birthday celebrations, allowing no other responsibilities or interruptions to deflect him from the appointed sacrifice. He was not erratic, irregular or inconsistent. These matters were of highest priority to him.

Job's Spiritual Perspective

From the character of Job's priesthood, we can learn seven things about his spiritual perspective. First, we see his determined resolution to lead his family in the worship of the living God. Nothing was going to keep him from his appointed duty.

Second, we see his sense of spiritual responsibility and loving care for the spiritual welfare of his children. A father who does not pray for his children and isn't burdened about their spiritual welfare is not doing his job.

Third, we also learn of Job's holy suspicion of his children's sinfulness. Family pride dies hard. We might say, "My kids wouldn't do that. They've been raised better than that!" But, Job discarded family pride, saying, "Perhaps my sons have sinned."

Fourth, we see Job's believing commitment to the divinely established public means of grace. God appointed that Job should use the means of sacrifice, so he was faithful to obey.

Fifth, we also see his confidence in those appointed means to meet the spiritual needs of his children. Sometimes Christians believe in everything that might do some good for kids except the means of grace God has appointed. It's not wrong to use all sorts of things to reach our children, but we should make sure we use what God has deemed best. He wants us to believe in his means of grace.

Sixth, we observe Job's assumption of his own spiritual authority to impose those means of grace on his children. He didn't let his kids rule the roost. He knew he had the right to command them to obey. Seventh, we see the earnest zeal of Job's spiritual leadership. How little enthusiasm do we often have to lead our families. May God give us such zeal!

The Continuation of Job's Priesthood

Job is the epitome of a man as a priest in his home. Yet, he lived in the Old Testament era of types and shadows. He offered physical sacrifices that have since been abrogated by the ultimate sacrifice of Christ. It may seem at first glance that his pattern should not apply to New Covenant Christians. However, there are several reasons that we should indeed imitate Job's model, even though we live under grace rather than law. First, Job's priesthood was not Levitical. He was not a Jew and did not live in the land of Palestine, so we cannot avoid his example by arguing that we are not of the tribe of Levi. Job himself was not a Levite.

Second, Job's priesthood was not covenantal. He did not exercise his priesthood because he was one of the patriarchs of Israel with whom God had established a special covenant, as in the cases of Abraham and Jacob. He was a Gentile, as are most of us.

Third, Job's priesthood was legal. His priestly activity is presented in Job 1 as an illustration of how he was "blameless, upright, fearing God and turning away from evil." The examples of Melchizedek, Noah and Jethro further justify his priestly actions. We cannot avoid the force of Job's example by claiming he was acting outside of God's established will.

Fourth, Job's priesthood was familial. The whole sphere of Job's priesthood as it is presented in Job 1 has to do with his family and children and nothing else. He was a priest because he was a father. If we have families and if we are fathers, we too are priests.

Fifth, Job's priesthood was original. Job's role preceded the Mosaic Covenant's restriction of priesthood to the tribe of Levi. His priesthood appears to have descended from an ancient conception of the husband and father as the head – and therefore the spiritual leader – of the family. The family (with the man as its head) was established at Creation, with burnt offerings introduced immediately after the fall of Adam. The family priesthood did not originate with the Old Covenant or even with the Abrahamic Covenant. So, we cannot assume that it passed away with the coming of the New Covenant.

Sixth, Job's priesthood was ceremonial. The idea of offering burnt offerings for sin originated with the fall of mankind into wrongdoing (Genesis 3:21; 4:4). Now that Jesus has conquered sin by his self-sacrifice, such typical sacrifices are no longer necessary. Although Christ's death means we no longer offer animal sacrifices on a family altar (as we will see later), it has not ended the headship of a man in his home. In particular, Job demonstrates that we are still responsible to lead our children to God through the great sacrifice offered by our Lord.

Seventh, Job's priesthood was primeval. Later in redemptive history, God restricted the offering of sacrifices to a central place and a chosen man. Further on, the gathered church replaced the temple as the place of God's special presence. These later institutions should not be viewed in opposition to the original priesthood of a man in his home. Rather, they work together with a man's priesthood. On one hand, we cannot abdicate our family priesthood to the church because we expect the church to be a substitute for our spiritual leadership in the home. On the other hand, we must not seek to apply our family priesthood in isolation from the church. We must strive to exercise our spiritual priesthood in harmony with the church, and see the two roles as complementary rather than threatening.

Application

So then, rather than avoiding Job's example as a priest, we must filter it through the work of Christ and apply it to our own lives.

Our Life's Priority -- No Excuses

Job's example demonstrates that every husband or father must make it a life priority to be a priest in his home. We will soon examine what the specific roles of such a priest are. By now, however, it should be abundantly clear that the role of a priest in the home is of the highest priority. Serving as a priest brings many demands upon men, who are often ready with their excuses. But Job's conduct teaches us that there are no adequate excuses for failing to fill this role. With his hectic life, it would have been easy for Job to shirk his duty by citing all the excuses we commonly use today. He had a large family, a vast business and enormous social responsibilities. But, he got the job done. He was a consistent spiritual leader who never missed his periodic offerings, no matter how early he had to get out of bed. Our excuses look awfully fragile in comparison with Job.

Our Spiritual Burden

Job also shows how the sheer necessity of the spiritual burden we feel for our family will drive us to become a priest in our home. The priority Job placed on his priesthood was rooted in the deep spiritual responsibility he felt for his children: "Perhaps my sons have sinned and cursed God in their hearts." We can often trace our failures as a priest in our home back to a significant lack of such concern.

This assumes, of course, the mantle of a priest doesn't depend on some exotic virtue only found in elite Christians. Rather, it's the fruit of very basic Christian affections in our heart. The natural desire for our children to be sanctified by converting grace should be sufficient to make us begin to act as a priest in our home. If we are characterized by drastic and continuing failures in this area, it is a powerful argument that we are not a Christian. At the least, if we know little or nothing of Job's burden to lead his family to the means of grace, his example is a compelling call to deep self-examination and repentance.

Hope for a Happy Family

For encouragement in the midst of this duty, Job's pattern also makes it clear that diligent spiritual leadership in the home can produce a happy, harmonious family. Job's family seems to have been a cheerful, close-knit bunch. Given that Job's wife later told her husband to curse God and die, the happiness of the family was probably not her doing. Ultimately, a cohesive and supportive family requires that a father be a strong, spiritual leader. A diligent mother may keep children under control when they are young, but if the father's steady hand isn't in evidence, the rebellion of older children can quickly lead to conflict and disharmony in the family. If we chose to abdicate our spiritual leadership through indifference, fear of conflict, busyness or any other excuse, we will eventually pay a stiff price.

A Priest Not Like Us

As men, we have a priest whom Job typifies. He also is blameless, but in a manner much higher than Job. He is holy, harmless, undefiled, exalted, separate from sinners. He never sinned in word, deed or nature. He had no need to say, "I have cleansed my heart."

This priest has a burden that is not simply like Job's, but is the source of Job's. His burden is expanded into transcendent perfection. This last Adam did not say, "*Perhaps* my sons have sinned," but "My sons *have* sinned." He ever lives to make intercession to those who come to God by him. He doesn't offer lambs or bulls to soothe an angry God as Job did. This priest became an offering himself. He was perfect humanity indwelt with perfect deity. As such, he was presented to God as a perfect sacrifice. No other sacrifice is needed to save the world. By looking to this priest, we can cast off our sins and ask God for the grace to become what Job was and more. Anyone who needs what this priest offers has only to ask. His grace is sufficient.

CHAPTER FOUR

A MAN AS AN INTERCESSOR
IN PRAYER

Most of us have probably been to an eye doctor. He asks you to read the eye chart, starting with the large letter "E" on top. Without your glasses or contacts, you might be able to read the first couple of rows, but the letters get fuzzier as you work your way down. You may see shapes, but they're hazy and indistinct. To determine your prescription, the doctor will then ask you to look through various sets of lenses. As he clicks through each lens and nears the strength that's right for your eyes, the letters slowly slide into better focus. When he reaches your ideal prescription, you can see everything with sharp, perfect clarity.

In the first three chapters, we've been bringing into focus the idea that a man should act as a priest in his home. We've considered the scriptural warrant for and classic portrait of such a man. Now, we'll sharpen the clarity of that picture by studying the special roles he should fulfill. Since men are to act as priests, we can learn much about their distinctive functions by studying the office of priest in Israel and throughout the Bible.

At the outset, we must realize that we should not even attempt to emulate several priestly roles. We don't offer burnt offerings upon family altars (unless we're particularly bad at grilling out). That work was first restricted to the Levitical priests in Israel, and then done away with through the once-for-all sacrifice of Christ. In addition, we are not ministers in God's holy temple. God also restricted this duty to the Levitical priests under the Old Covenant.

Still, priests fulfilled five distinctive roles in the Bible that we must carry out in our home. Priests are intercessors in prayer, directors in worship, mediators of divine blessing, instructors in scripture and judges in holy things. We'll consider the first of these roles in this chapter.

Intercession

First of all, a man as a priest in his home should serve as an intercessor in prayer. Men are to be engaged constantly in the work of prayer. Most Christian men know this. But, we should be practicing more than just general prayer. We should also be active in the specific form of prayer known as intercession – that is, petitioning God on behalf of the needs of others. Specifically, men ought to intercede for the needs of their families and households. It's amazing how selfish we can be even in spiritual things and how much of our prayer time we spend on ourselves. The Bible, in contrast, teaches that we must also pray for others. Let's take a look at several biblical proofs for the man's role as an intercessor in his home.

Job as an Intercessor

As we saw in the last chapter, Job acts as an intercessor for his children. In Job 42:8, God says to Job's friends, "Now therefore, take for yourselves seven bulls and seven rams, and go to My servant Job, and offer up a burnt offering for yourselves, and My servant Job will pray for you. For I will accept him so that I may not do with you according to your folly, because you have not spoken of Me what is right, as My servant Job has." This is the account of Job's vindication, not only in terms of his wealth and prosperity, but in regard to his friends. In asking Job to offer these burnt offerings – the very kind of burnt offerings he brought for his children in Job 1:5 – these three men also expected Job to intercede before God on their behalf. When someone offers burnt offerings in the Bible, there is an intimate connection between the smoke symbolically rising from the altar and the prayer of the one who is making that offering. The word offering means *"to make to go up."* The offerings are a symbolic prayer.

In Job 42:8 we are told explicitly that Job should accompany his burnt offerings with intercessory prayer. It is impossible to think that he would have accompanied these offerings with prayer and would have neglected to do the same when he offered sacrifices for his own children. Job was a man who said, "Perhaps my sons have sinned and cursed God in their heart." He was also a man who rose early to offer sacrifices every time the occasion demanded it. We cannot reasonably think that such a man would simply go through the form of offering sacrifices for his children, or that he would not accompany the sacrifices with his own prayers. The logical conclusion is that such intercessory prayer was an integral part of Job's priestly offerings for his children.

Israelite Priests as Intercessors

The intimate relationship between Job's offerings and his prayers prepares us to see that the priests in Israel – the supreme example of those who offered sacrifices – should also be regarded as intercessors for Israel. It is not surprising, therefore, to find priests' offerings and prayers spoken of together, as in Ezra 6:9-10:

> Whatever is needed, both young bulls, rams, and lambs for a burnt offering to the God of heaven, and wheat, salt, wine and anointing oil, as the priests in Jerusalem request, it is to be given to them daily without fail, that they may offer acceptable sacrifices to the God of heaven and pray for the life of the king and his sons.

The passage refers to a decree of King Darius with regard to restoration of the temple and sacrifices in the land of Judah that was now part of his empire. Even a pagan in that culture commonly assumed that when priests offered sacrifices they would also pray for the ones who had given those sacrifices – in this case, the king and his sons.

We also see this intercessory work of the priests of Israel in regard to offerings (particularly incense offerings) elsewhere in the Old Testament. God instructed the priests to place incense offerings on the golden altar at the screen that guarded the Holy of Holies. They could go there frequently to offer an incense offering. They were not limited to just once a year as with the Holy of Holies itself. These incense offerings were regarded as symbolic of prayer.

Hebrews 9:3-4 links the two things in its account of an incense offering: "Behind the second veil there was a tabernacle, which is called the Holy of Holies, having a golden altar of incense and the ark of the covenant covered on all sides with gold, in which was a golden jar holding the manna, and Aaron's rod which budded, and the tables of the covenant." Accounts in the Old Testament reveal that the golden altar of incense (a place of prayer) was not actually in the Holy of Holies, but was so closely associated with it that the writer of Hebrews could say it was part of the area. This place of prayer was integral to the sacrificial process.

More evidence that prayers are intertwined with offerings comes in Revelation 5:8, "When He had taken the book, the four living creatures and the twenty-four elders fell down before the Lamb, each one holding a harp and golden bowls full of incense, which are the prayers of the saints." Again in Revelation 8:3-4, John writes:

> Another angel came and stood at the altar, holding a golden censer; and much incense was given to him, so that he might add it to the prayers of all the saints on the golden altar which was before the throne. And the smoke of the incense, with the prayers of the saints, went up before God out of the angel's hand.

John clearly saw the figurative significance of the incense offering as symbolizing the prayers of the saints.

In the gospel of Luke, we find the figurative and literal offerings combining during the worship of the temple. Luke 1:9-11 says:

> According to the custom of the priestly office, he [Zacharias] was chosen by lot to enter the temple of the Lord and burn incense. And the whole multitude of the people were in prayer outside at the hour of the incense offering. And an angel of the Lord appeared to him, standing to the right of the altar of incense.

See the picture? Zacharias is burning incense before the Lord, right on the brink of the Holy of Holies. The people of Israel gathered outside know the significance of this moment. This is the appropriate hour for them to offer their prayers, while the priest offers the incense as a symbol of those prayers. This is a beautiful association and we learn from this that the Israelite priests' special roles included that of intercessor.

Christ as an Intercessor

The third biblical proof for this role is that Jesus Christ, our great high priest, is peculiarly an intercessor. Our Lord's high priestly intercessions for us in heaven are explicitly stated in two New Testament passages. Romans 8:34 says, "Who is the one who condemns? Christ Jesus is He who died, yes, rather who was raised, who is at the right hand of God, who also intercedes for us." Additionally, Hebrews 7:25 says, "Therefore He is able also to save forever those who draw near to God through Him, since He always lives to make intercession for them."

Intercession is what our Lord is doing in heaven now. He has once-for-all offered himself a sacrifice for men, and he now sits at the Father's right hand, pleading continually on behalf of his people. The word translated *intercede* in these passages may also be variously translated as *approach, appeal, petition* or *pray.* Whichever English word is used, it portrays our Lord as constantly engaged in the work of intercessory prayer. Since in Ephesians 5:25, Paul tells husbands to love their wives as Christ loved the church, and since Christ's work as a priest (sanctifying and cleansing) occupies Paul's thoughts, it is not far-fetched to suggest that Christ's priestly work of intercession should serve as a pattern for our love towards our wife and children. This is part of what Paul had in mind when he told us to emulate Christ's behavior.

Though these arguments are helpful, they simply underscore what the light of nature and sanctified common sense should already teach Christian men. How can we possibly claim to be the heads, providers, guides and protectors of our families if we neglect the most important method of assuring their welfare – the means of intercessory prayer? Our duties as the heads of our homes necessarily include interceding for our families.

Application

With the biblical proofs for a man as a priest in his home as a foundation, we come to several practical lessons for men. How does intercession play out in everyday life? What specific things can a man do to bless his family through prayer? How should he pray?

Priest Intercedes Sacrificially

First, we should intercede sacrificially, praying in explicit association with a sacrifice we have offered. This was how Job interceded and it was also the method of intercession for the priests in Israel. The king gave them sacrifices expecting them to pray in conjunction with those sacrifices. The principle is also true of our Lord's intercession. His sacrifice is the basis upon which he now appears before the throne of grace. And so when we come to pray as priests in our home, the question naturally arises: "Where is my sacrifice? How can I pray without a sacrifice to accompany my intercession?"

Thankfully, we don't have to worry about finding animals to sacrifice. Instead, we should look immediately to the work of the Lord Jesus Christ. We come to intercede on the basis of his great sacrifice that "He did once for all when He offered up Himself" (Hebrews 7:27). We don't intercede on the basis of how faithful we've been as husbands, how good we've been as Christians or how careful we've been in our duties. We come to intercede for our families on the basis of the effectual blood of Jesus Christ, and we must never forget that.

This concept is a helpful encouragement and pointed reminder when we come before Christ in our priestly identity. Do we come boldly to the mercy-seat, pleading the merits of Christ's blood? We won't if we're bringing our own deeds, our own precise duties that we've accomplished. We won't approach confidently if we think we can love our wives faithfully and raise our children wisely on our own. We'll only advance boldly to the mercy-seat of God if we come with the blood of Christ washing over our hands in the golden bowl of the Father's love.

A Priest Intercedes Specifically

A priest also intercedes particularly, or specifically. We may not have ever thought about this, but every priest in the Bible is for certain people. It's one of the reasons the doctrine of particular redemption makes sense. Offering sacrifices is the work of a priest, and a priest in the Bible is always the priest for particular people. He prays for the same people that he offers sacrifices for. Job offered sacrifices for his children and interceded particularly for them; just as he also did for his three friends. By his death, Christ offered himself up for his chosen people. Now, "He is able also to save forever those who draw near to God through Him, since He always lives to make intercession for them" (Hebrews 7:25). John 17:9 also reminds us that Christ prays particularly for His people, "I do not ask on behalf of the world, but of those whom You have given Me."

Intercession means that a man as a priest in his home should pray particularly for his wife, his children and the needs of his household. We ought to pray for other matters as well. But, whatever else may remain undone in our prayer life, we must pray particularly and with a special focus for our wife and children. We should bring their salvation, their spiritual needs and their temporal needs before Christ daily.

If we do not pray for them, we should feel guilty. This is a sin for which we need to seek the forgiveness of God; a sin for which we need a priest. How can we stand in the light of Scripture – and even in the light of our own consciences – and deny our wives and our children the most effectual means for their welfare? In interceding for our families, we must be like the Christ of whom we sing, "My name from the palms of his hands, eternity will not erase/Impressed on his heart it remains, in marks of indelible grace." As our names are impressed on the heart of the Savior, the names of our wives and children must be indelibly impressed on our hearts so that we cannot pray without bearing them before the throne of grace.

A Priest Intercedes Consistently

Third, a family priest intercedes consistently. The language of great consistency permeates biblical passages on priestly intercession: "Thus Job did continually . . . Far be it from me that I should cease to pray for you . . . He always lives to make intercession for them." Two things, at least, are included in such consistency. We should pray *regularly* for those over whom we have responsibility. In fact, we should not be satisfied with ourselves if we do not pray for our family by name every day. Consistency also means that we should pray with *perseverance*. Legitimate hindrances may keep us from the place of daily prayer, but such hindrances simply demand perseverance rather than capitulation and compromise. Our wives and children may even provoke us and tempt us to stop praying for them, but these things should draw us again and again to the mercy-seat. Even years of hard-heartedness from our children should not blunt our efforts. The sovereignty of the throne of grace and the power of the blood of Christ must make us say, "Far be it from me that I should cease to pray for you."

A Priest Intercedes With Sensitivity

A priest should also intercede with sensitivity. Hebrews 5:2 says of the high priest, "He can deal gently with the ignorant and misguided, since he himself also is beset with weakness." The verse is referring to what we call sensitivity in our day. While our culture often thinks of sensitive men as weak, our Lord Himself is a compassionate and sensitive high priest, as it says in Hebrews 4:15: "For we do not have a high priest who cannot sympathize with our weaknesses, but One who has been tempted in all things as we are, yet without sin."

Sensitivity like this will lead to discernment with regard to the spiritual needs and sins of our families. Job was perceptive in this way. He knew that even legitimate celebrating and feasting could be the occasion of grievous sins. Although he may not have actually seen anything sinful, he said, "*Perhaps* my sons have sinned and cursed God in their hearts."

Men are proverbial for needing to learn sensitivity because most of us are relatively block-headed and self-centered by nature. Television sitcoms often strike comedic gold with extreme cases of self-absorbed, inconsiderate men. But, this stereotype is a tragedy of the biblical ideal. To intercede rightly for our families, we must ask God for deliverance from our native indifference and insensitivity. But it's more than just asking for help. We must work at it. An earnest and determined embrace of our duty to be priestly intercessors for our families will help us develop this grace.

So what will make us discerning and perceptive? Here again, we come to one of those truths which flattens us in terms of our pride and our excuses. A discerning and perceptive nature results from nothing more elaborate than simply loving the people we're concerned about. True love makes us sensitive and therefore willing and able to meet the needs of our wife and children. If we care about our families, we'll pay attention to them. We'll file away mental notes about what our wives like and dislike. We'll make an effort to learn our children's tastes. We'll find out what issues they're dealing with at home and at school. Then, in both prayer and action, we'll make use of the intelligence we've gathered.

Sensitive priests will do this for their families because of a yearning heart that desires their families to be close to Christ. Insensitive men are mostly concerned with themselves, so they neglect their families. Once we begin to biblically love our family and take our responsibility to intercede for them seriously, we will become discerning. It may be hard going and it may be very gradual, but we will make progress. We'll grow in our understanding of what our wife and children need. We'll even ask how we can best pray for them. Nothing less than this kind of serious concern and love will increase our sensitivity to our family.

A Priest Intercedes Earnestly

That brings us to the final point: a priest intercedes earnestly. When Job prayed for his children, he most likely did not just automatically mumble a few words that he had repeated countless times before.

We know he rose up early in the morning to ask for mercy for sins his children *might* have committed. Surely Job prayed earnestly for his children, just as all true priests pour out their hearts to the God of heaven.

How often does intercession for our wives and children merely become part of the dreary routine of our prayer life? We tell other people what a wonderful wife we have and how hard she works, but if she is so burdened, why don't we pray for her more? If we're so appreciative, why don't we give her the gift of prayer? If our children stand in need of salvation, have we ever prayed and fasted for them? Do our children need direction concerning education, college, vocation or spouse? These momentous decisions face them at a time in their lives when they may not be ready to make them. We should cry to the Lord for wisdom for our children.

Because of our native sinfulness, the role of an intercessor in prayer can create a heavy burden for men to bear. A sense of weakness and inadequacy can weigh us down, along with guilt at failing in our task. Some of us have to confess to the Lord that we've failed miserably to pray as we should have for our wives and children. We must ask for grace to fulfill our calling as priests.

A Cure for Our Guilt

But when our guilt threatens to overwhelm us, we must not despair. There is always hope because we have a better priest than ourselves praying for us. Remember the words of Hebrews 10:21, "We have a great priest over the house of God." If Christ's example teaches us that we must pray for our families, it also teaches us that he prays for his family. If his example shows us that we must attempt to effectively pray down blessing on our families, it also demonstrates that he sovereignly prays down blessings on his own family. And here's the supremely comforting part: Christ's prayers are always heard. He prays for us as a part of his family, that we might pray for our own families. Thinking of this will help lighten the sense of inadequacy and guilt we have, and enable us to begin to pray as we should. What a great God we serve!

If you are an unconverted father who is struggling with the tensions of life, this truth may be exactly what you need to set you on the road to salvation. If you feel like you need someone to pray for you, you're right. You do need someone to pray for you. Here is what the gospel offers you: On the basis of what he accomplished on the cross, an all-sufficient Savior ever lives to make intercession for those who come to God by him. He will pray for you as you're struggling, but you must come out of your sins and draw near to God through Christ. You cannot go to God or even pray to him without Jesus Christ. Without Christ, not even your best efforts are acceptable; your worship and prayers are an abomination. But the good news – the incredibly gracious, never-ending good news – is that Christ ever lives to make intercession for those who come to God through him. Go to Jesus Christ now and ask him to pray for you. He will pray, and his prayers will do more than you could ever imagine.

CHAPTER FIVE

A MAN AS A DIRECTOR
OF RELIGIOUS WORSHIP

With every year that passes, the power of examples in our lives becomes clearer. We often find ourselves responding to a situation in exactly the same way our fathers responded hundreds of times before us. Many of us have other significant examples – pastors, teachers, friends – that have shaped us profoundly. As we see our children imitate us for better or for worse, the enormous influence of our example on our children also becomes increasingly apparent.

This extraordinary power of example gives great significance to the topic of this book. A large part of the book's purpose is to show to husbands and fathers the priests in the Bible who stand out as mighty examples in the roles they play. In this chapter, we'll look at the second of these roles – the man as a director of religious worship.

Throughout the Bible, the priest appears as the one who ministers to the Lord and officiates during worship. Therefore, he exercises administrative authority over matters of religious worship. In the language of the contemporary church, he is a worship leader. We'll examine this role of a priest, once again, by looking at the models of Job, the priests of Israel and our great high priest, the Lord Jesus Christ.

Job as a Director of Religious Worship

We can observe Job's leadership in the worship of his family by re-reading Job 1:5:

> When the days of feasting had completed their cycle, Job would send and consecrate them, rising up early in the morning and offering burnt offerings according to the number of them all; for

Job said, 'Perhaps my sons have sinned and cursed God in their hearts.' Thus Job did continually.

Clearly, Job used his initiative and leadership to gather his family together for periodic sacrifices by which he committed them to the care of God. The key words are "Job would send and consecrate them." This simple phrase implies volumes about Job's leadership in his home. He exercised the prerogative of requiring his children's presence in the religious worship he intended to conduct. He didn't invite them or ask their permission. He simply sent and sanctified them. Job was unmistakably a godly, assertive director of religious worship in his home.

Priests of Israel as Directors of Religious Worship

This is one of those facts that is assumed everywhere in the Old Testament without being explicitly stated in any individual passage. We'll look, then, at a number of passages where the role of priests in Israel as the administrators of religious worship is evident.

Deuteronomy 17:12, 18 says, "The man who acts presumptuously by not listening to the priest who stands there to serve the LORD your God, nor to the judge, that man shall die; thus you shall purge the evil from Israel...Now it shall come about when he sits on the throne of his kingdom, he shall write for himself a copy of this law on a scroll in the presence of the Levitical priests." In other words, the priests were there to serve the Lord and to direct on the occasion of copying the law.

Joshua 22:13 describes the action the nation of Israel took in the case of Achan, "Then the sons of Israel sent to the sons of Reuben and to the sons of Gad and to the half-tribe of Manasseh, into the land of Gilead, Phinehas the son of Eleazar the priest." Here's a matter of religious importance – a widely-known potential case of idolatry. Phinehas the high priest is sent to judge the circumstances because he was the director of religious worship in Israel.

First Kings 4:1-2 says, "Now King Solomon was king over all Israel. These were his officials: Azariah the son of Zadok was the priest." Just as the President of the United States has his cabinet to advise him, Solomon had his cabinet as well. Azariah the priest was his secretary of religion. It was he who was presented as the director of religious worship in Israel.

Second Chronicles 19:8-11 reads in part:

> In Jerusalem also Jehoshaphat appointed some of the Levites and priests, and some of the heads of the fathers' households of Israel, for the judgment of the LORD and to judge disputes among the inhabitants of Jerusalem. Then he charged them saying, 'Thus you shall do in the fear of the LORD, faithfully and wholeheartedly...Behold, Amariah the chief priest will be over you in all that pertains to the LORD.'

Amariah the chief priest was the director of religious worship in Israel. Amariah was the one who would oversee spiritual matters.

Second Chronicles 23:8 says, "...the Levites and all Judah did according to all that Jehoiada the priest commanded." The Levites and the members of the tribe of Judah acted according to the command of the priest. They did not according to their own desires.

Several passages in Acts pertain to the subject, including Acts 5:27; 7:1; 9:1-2; 22:5 and 23:1-5. In these verses, we learn that the high priest was the head of the Sanhedrin of Israel. When the persecutor Saul planned to go to Damascus to arrest Christians there, he sought letters from this high priest. Throughout the book, it's clear that the high priest of Israel exercised leadership over Israel, not only in the temple and in Judea, but even in the far-flung synagogues of the Diaspora. Paul especially emphasizes this in Acts 23:1-5.

There are two crucial lessons to carry away from these passages. First, the priests in Israel possessed a real authority in the nation. Second, this authority had to do specifically with the religious worship of the people.

Jesus Christ as a Director of Religious Worship

We learn from the New Testament that the Lord Jesus Christ is "a great high priest over the house of God" (Hebrews 10:21). Even though very few Christians today recognize Christ's priesthood over the church, his will ought to direct what goes on in the church. No matter how many Christians think they're allowed to invent worship as they go, the Bible teaches that Jesus Christ alone, as a priest over the house of God, has the authority to direct our worship.

Several other passages in the book of Hebrews emphasize this authority of Christ over the religious worship of his people. Hebrews 3:1 identifies Christ as the sent one of God and the high priest of his confessing people when it says, "Therefore, holy brethren, partakers of a heavenly calling, consider Jesus, the Apostle and High Priest of our confession." Hebrews 5:4-5 adds, "And no one takes the honor to himself, but receives it when he is called by God, even as Aaron was. So also Christ did not glorify Himself so as to become a high priest, but He who said to Him, 'You are my son, today I have begotten you.'" God – the omnipotent creator of the universe – was the one who made his Son Jesus Christ a high priest.

When we combine the biblical arguments that the priest is a director of religious worship with the teaching of the Bible that a man is a priest in his home, we must draw a very clear deduction: As priests in our home, we should feel a special responsibility to be the leader and initiator of religious worship for our household. Even without this argument, we might have gleaned the conclusion from a careful and spiritual consideration of our headship as men. Surely, if we are the head of the home, we must particularly be so in the religious sphere. This means that as the leader, we must give direction to our family in the worship of God.

Yet, this conclusion is sadly lost on many men who boast of their headship in the home, but never lead their families in worship. Considering men's headship through the priestly glasses given to us by the Scriptures should make the matter clear even to fallen minds such as ours. We must exercise initiative and leadership with regard to the religious worship of our households.

Application

This conclusion leads to four applications regarding personal worship, family worship, public worship and the day of worship. We'll trace these applications out in the remainder of the chapter, considering all of this in the light of our great high priest above.

As men, we must exercise leadership with regard to the personal worship of each member of our family.

We must be concerned that each member of our family not only come to know the Lord, but also consistently engage in the personal disciplines of Bible study and private prayer – the personal worship of the living God. True worship begins only when a sinner bows in submission to Christ (John 4:21-24). If we are to be the director of religious worship in our home, we must privately engage our children in conversation about their souls, seeking to bring them to a genuine knowledge of their sins and God's grace. We must not leave this duty to the pastor or our wife alone. Our child or teenager may try to stiff-arm us when we bring up spiritual realities. But as God's appointed representative to them, we must be caring enough to be faithful to their souls.

This also means that as fathers, we must make sure that our children, at the appropriate age, develop the holy habit of spending part of each day in private prayer and the study of their Bibles. We must oversee our children to make sure they are practicing these disciplines. We must talk with our wife to make sure she is keeping a good conscience by having daily times of private devotions. We may have to deny ourselves so that we can organize our home in such a way that makes it easy to worship God on a daily basis. This calls for spiritual-mindedness, careful domestic management and good communication so that these crucial disciplines are not driven out of the lives of our wife or children by worldly pressures.

Some may object that we shouldn't teach unconverted children to pray and read their Bibles. Rather, they suggest we should delay those practices until they can be shown as proof that the children have been converted. However, prayer and Bible study are a duty of nature, not something that Christians only are entitled to. *The 1689 Baptist Confession of Faith* (22:3) says that prayer, with thanksgiving, "being one part of natural worship, is by God required of all men." We require even our unconverted children to worship God during public church services each week. Why should anything be different about personal worship? Pressing these duties upon children may also provide them with many beneficial influences. Their lack of desire to read the Bible and pray may awaken them to their unconverted state. And, such times of daily prayer and Bible reading may end up being the means God uses to convert them.

We should also be careful about jumping to conclusions concerning the spiritual condition of children. Just because they're small doesn't mean they're unconverted. They very well may be trusting in Christ. If nothing else, daily prayer and Bible study – like all good habits – should be ingrained at a young age so that when children are converted, they won't struggle with having their devotions consistently.

We must exercise leadership with regard to family worship.

The Bible assumes that it is the duty of every head of a household to gather his family together regularly to worship the living God. This is not the place for a full-blown treatment of family worship. But, every Christian husband and father ought to believe that it is his obligation to lead his family in domestic worship. The mere fact that a man is a priest in his home should sufficiently suggest that this kind of leadership is his responsibility.

Family worship doesn't have to be a complicated process. As men, we should think through what we want to say. And, even though life is hectic, we should carve out a few minutes to gather the kids and their mom before the throne of grace. After dinner might be a good time to schedule family worship. Another opportunity may be just before the kids head to bed for the night. A brief time of singing, praying and short instruction from God's Word is enough to direct the family's attention to the God who created them. Such times can also be invaluable training for children who are learning to sit through a church service.

As men, we must ask ourselves how we can think of ourselves as priests in our home if we are not conducting consistent family worship. If a man is a priest, he is a leader of worship. Where is that worship? The Bible charges us to bring our children up in the discipline and instruction of the Lord. It also says that men are responsible to teach their children. One of the best places for teaching to occur is in family worship. This worship is a vital plank in the foundation of a man's priesthood in the home.

We must exercise leadership with regard to the public worship of God.

In Job's day – before the Mosaic Covenant – there was no appointed public worship of God. Job lived prior to the time in which a special place (Jerusalem) and a special priesthood (the sons of Aaron) were chosen in Israel. Now that God has established his worship in the church – an institution distinct from the family – our situation is different than that of Job. In this day, we exercise our priesthood in connection and with the support of the ordained public worship of God.

We should not resent or neglect the church as if it were competing with our priesthood. Some churches may unjustly vie for needed family time if they multiply stated meetings and functions that would interfere with the integrity of the family. The church must recognize this and not undermine a man's leadership of his family. But some men have developed such a jealousy for their leadership in their homes that they have begun to view the church as somehow interfering with their headship. Some object to Sunday Schools where the church endeavors to systematically instruct children in the Scriptures because this takes control out of their hands. Some families have even become so insensitive to the divine ordinance of the church and public worship that they worship in their own homes – perhaps with one or two other families – without claiming to be a church. This is clearly a violation of the Scriptures.

Such conduct often flows from an insensitive individualism that fails to appreciate how God has restricted the family priesthood through the appointment of his public worship. After public worship was instituted in Israel, family priests were obliged to enter into that worship. Today, God commands priests and their families not to forsake the assembling of themselves together with the church (Hebrews 10:25).

The church in turn does not oppose family priesthood. Rather, it supports and supplements the family as men exercise their priesthood in the context of and in harmony with the local church. We must wholeheartedly support the public worship of our church as part of our priesthood. We should stand behind the church's pastors and worship. Then, in our homes, we must endeavor in every way possible to support and promote the legitimate ministries of the church.

It is our duty to lead our family to the public worship of God. We ought to arrange our own schedule and that of our family so we can together attend the church's public worship and prayer meetings (unless providentially hindered). Our family should feel holy pressure from us that will make them think twice about missing a meeting of the church.

We must exercise leadership with regard to the day of worship -- the Lord's Day.

God has always given his people a weekly day of worship. From creation to the resurrection of Christ, that Sabbath fell on the seventh-day of the week. Since Christ's resurrection on a Sunday, we have celebrated the Lord's Day Sabbath on the first day of the week. This Sabbath is a day of rest from our ordinary labors, recreations and employments. It is to be kept holy to the Lord for the purposes of public and private worship. *The 1689 Baptist Confession of Faith* teaches this in Chapter 22:7-8:

> As it is a law of nature, applicable to all, that a proportion of time, determined by God, should be allocated for the worship of God, so, by His Word, He has particularly appointed one day in seven to be kept as a holy Sabbath to Himself. The commandment to this effect is positive, moral, and of perpetual application. It is binding upon all men in all ages. From the beginning of the world to the resurrection of Christ the Sabbath

was the last day of the week, but when Christ's resurrection took place it was changed to the first day of the week, which is called the Lord's day. It is to be continued to the world's end as the Christian Sabbath, the observance of the seventh day being abolished.

Men keep the Sabbath holy to the Lord when, having duly prepared their hearts and settled their mundane affairs beforehand, for the sake of the Lord's command they set aside all works, words and thoughts that pertain to their worldly employment and recreations, and devote the whole of the Lord's day to the public and private exercises of God's worship, and to duties of necessity and mercy.

Observing this day of rest will naturally promote the personal, family and public worship of God. That's why it's so important to a man of God in his home. An entire day away from television, work, sports and other worldly distractions creates a perfect space in our busy lives which we can easily fill with talking and worshiping together. The neglect of this day will make it easier to marginalize those types of worship.

It is especially a man's duty to see that he and his household observe the day. Both the Old and New Testaments teach that there is a day of worship that is to be kept to the Lord. Exodus 20:8-11 says:

Remember the Sabbath day, to keep it holy. Six days you shall labor and do all your work, but the seventh day is a Sabbath of the LORD your God; in it you shall not do any work, you or your son or your daughter, your male or your female servant or your cattle or your sojourner who stays with you. For in six days the LORD made the heavens and the earth, the sea and all that is in them, and rested on the seventh day; therefore the LORD blessed the Sabbath day and made it holy.

Each of the Ten Commandments – including the fourth commandment – is especially addressed to men as the heads of households. The tenth commandment makes this clear. Therefore, as the head of the home, we must encourage the observance of the fourth commandment by promoting spiritual, God-glorifying activities and discouraging anything that would interfere with the great opportunities God has given us on this day.

Here then, are a few encouragements to help us as the head of our household to persevere in keeping the Lord's Day holy. We have this wonderful gift of a whole day to spend in the exercise of public and private worship. We should use it. The worship of God is a blessed event that true Christians enjoy, so nothing should hinder us from the place of public worship. We should make sure that our whole family is at Sunday School and morning and evening worship. Around the lunch table, we can discuss what the children learned in Sunday School and the main points of the pastor's sermon.

To occupy the rest of the afternoon, we could review assigned memory verses with our children and talk with them about what the verses mean. We could give an older child a good book to read and then discuss it with him or her. We could choose one of our children each week, lay down with him or her for their nap, and use that time to talk about the gospel, Christ and the state of his or her soul. It's one thing for children to see their dad go to church; it's quite another to see him come into their room, lie down on their bed and talk to them about eternal things. We could also take our children on a walk or to light up the faces of old folks with a visit to a nursing home. Then at the end of the Lord's Day, as the family eats dinner or a snack, we could draw our children out by asking them to share something from the day that especially sticks in their mind.

The possibilities the Lord's Day gives us are endless if we see the day for the joy and privilege it is, rather than a restrictive day designed to strip all pleasure away. God has given us a tremendous opportunity if we will take seriously our responsibility to lead our families in observing his day. May God grant us grace through his Son, the great high priest, to heed these things, confess our sins, receive strength for the good of our families, and finally, to do these things for his glory.

CHAPTER SIX
A MAN AS A MEDIATOR
OF DIVINE BLESSING

A well-known text of Scripture reads, "For there is one God, and one mediator also between God and men, the man Christ Jesus" (1 Timothy 2:5). The hymn-writer puts it this way:

> Jesus, my great high priest, offered his blood and died
> My guilty conscience seeks no sacrifice beside
> His powerful blood did once atone
> And now it pleads before the throne.

Though there is only one Mediator between God and men, here on earth there are many types and shadows of the great Mediator. One such symbol is a man who is a husband and father in his home. In this chapter, we'll consider that man's special priestly role as a mediator of divine blessing to his family. The roles we've looked at so far have been full of reminders of the duties men face. We should come to this chapter with hearts full of faith in the Mediator who enables us to fulfill those duties and who calls us to reflect his blessings to those in our homes.

In the New Testament, the Greek word translated with the English word mediator is used six times. This word is derived from the Greek word for middle. Thus, a mediator is literally the man in the middle. This word is used twice of Moses, who was the go-between connecting God and the nation of Israel (Galatians 3:19-20). The same word is used four times of Christ (1 Timothy 2:5; Hebrews 8:6; 9:15; 12:24). The Hebrews passages especially show that Christ functioned as a mediator in his priestly capacity. By definition, priests stand in the gap between holy God and sinful man. Hebrews 5:1 says they are "appointed on behalf of men in things pertaining to God." A mediator, then, is one who is a channel or conduit of blessing. A mediator is like the man on the old TV show The Millionaire who delivered the checks to those whom his millionaire employer wanted to give one million dollars. The recipients were not given the checks by the millionaire, but by his mediator. So also it is through Christ that all the blessings of the New Covenant come to those whom God has chosen.

Evidence for Men as Mediators of Divine Blessing

In some respects this is the most difficult of the five roles of a priest to apply to a man in his home. Speaking of men as mediators of divine blessing does not equate their mediatorial character with that of Christ. But, there are principles that apply in both cases. Consider the following five arguments in favor of a man as a mediator of divine blessing in his home:

Job attempted to mediate spiritual blessings to his children by offering sacrifices on their behalf.

In Job 1:5, he offered sacrifices to satisfy any divine vengeance due his children for cursing God in their hearts. If successful, his actions would have resulted in the opposite of cursing. He would have brought divine blessing upon his children. Thus, those actions which Job initiated as the priest of his home would have been the channel of blessing to his family.

The patriarchs who were priests in their homes mediated divine blessings to their children by pronouncing effectual blessings upon them.

Several passages in the book of Genesis show the patriarchs blessing their children (Genesis 9:24-27 [Noah]; 27:1-28:3 [Isaac]; 48:1-20 and 49:1, 28 [Israel]). In these passages, Noah, Isaac and Jacob were exercising a power and privilege forbidden to ordinary men. The blessings with which they blessed their children came ultimately from the Spirit of prophecy which dwelt within them. We cannot apply the patriarchs' privileged position or prophetic spirit to ourselves, but we still may glean several items of great importance from them and other prominent Old Testament men.

First, their pattern instructs us that we ought to aspire to be a source of blessing for our wives and children. In 2 Samuel 6:20 and 1 Chronicles 16:43, David's heart compelled him to bless his household as he returned from the place of worship. Can we say the same? Do we leave church more determined than ever to be a blessing to our families?

Second, their example teaches us to speak in a positive and encouraging way to our wives and children whenever we can. These men prophetically pronounced a blessing upon their children. They actually spoke it. It is so easy to be negative in what we say, especially when we have to correct our children over and over again. Because of this, we've got to make a concerted effort to encourage them as much as possible. We want our families to remember how much we blessed them, both verbally and through the Scriptures.

Third, just as the patriarchs understood their children, we should attempt to recognize the peculiar gifts and talents God has given to our children. When properly developed and sanctified, these gifts may be a channel of divine blessing. Jacob typifies this when he blesses each of his sons with the "blessing appropriate to him" in Genesis 49. These blessings did not result exclusively from the Spirit of prophecy. There was a direct correlation between the clearly manifested character of his sons and the attendant blessings Jacob bestowed on them. We too should attempt to point our children in the path of blessing which will best fit their particular natures. They will find encouragement as they develop their gifts so that they may be blessed by God.

There is tremendous evidence throughout the Old Testament that the blessing of God's people was one of the preeminent responsibilities of the priests in Israel

The sheer weight of emphasis in the Old Testament should be enough to convince us. Deuteronomy 21:5, a representative sample, says, "Then the priests, the sons of Levi, shall come near, for the

L<small>ORD</small> your God has chosen them to serve Him and to blessing the name of the L<small>ORD</small>." Other passages include Leviticus 9:22-24; Numbers 6:22-27; Deuteronomy 21:5; 1 Chronicles 23:13; 2 Chronicles 30:27; 2 Chronicles 6:41; and Psalm 132:16.

As the priests in Israel were to bless God's people, so we in our own houses are to bless our families. Deuteronomy 21:5 equates serving God with blessing people in his name. Psalm 132:16 says that priests are clothed in salvation – the purpose of which is to bring God's salvation down to the people. If one of the foremost responsibilities of a priest is to bless his people, then as priests, we should proclaim blessings in our home.

Our great high priest is a mediator of divine blessing for us, his church (Genesis 14:19; Luke 24:50-51; Hebrews 7:22; 8:6).

The Luke 24 passage records Jesus' final moments on earth with his disciples. As he blessed them, he lifted up his hands and the Spirit took him up to heaven. The last the disciples saw of Jesus, his hands were raised as he pronounced a spoken blessing upon them. Surely our Lord Jesus Christ was a blessing priest, and if he is an example for us, we must strive to pronounce the same types of blessings on our families.

We know from the direct teaching of Scripture that a man as the head of his home will bring either divine blessing or cursing upon his home, depending on his own character and conduct.

This is a weighty, serious and even difficult teaching. But, it is one we must face as men. Just as the priests mediated the divine blessing to Israel (or the divine curse, as in the case of Eli's sons), and just as the Lord perfectly mediates the divine blessing to his people, so a man as a priest in his home to some degree mediates either the divine blessing or cursing to his home.

Some have taken this scriptural fact as an argument for baptizing their infants. They believe they can somehow mediate covenantal status or a saving blessing to their children in a way that qualifies them for baptism. However, the scriptural assertion that a man affects his home through his actions should in no way be construed to mean that a man should confer the New Covenant sign of baptism upon his children. Many of the children of a godly man will experience great blessing through the channel of their father. But, there is no scriptural justification for proclaiming through baptism that the infants of a godly man have already experienced the greatest blessing of all, salvation. That is, after all, what we're saying when we baptize babies. We are proclaiming to the world that salvation belongs to them. Nowhere, though, does Scripture teach that the sign of baptism applies to infants unable to believe on their own.

But though it is no argument for infant baptism, there is a doctrine of house-solidarity in the Bible, particularly in the book of Proverbs. This doctrine teaches that a man's conduct profoundly influences the welfare of his house or family. Psalm 112:1-2 clearly shows this: "Praise the Lord! How blessed is the man who fears the Lord, who greatly delights in his commandments. His descendants will be mighty on earth; the generation of the upright will be blessed." Proverbs 3:33; 11:29; 12:7; 14:11; 15:6, 25, 27; 17:13 and 21:12 build on this same reality.

Add to this the clearly stated duty of a man to be the head and savior of his wife (Ephesians 5:23-29). We are to be our wife's nourisher, preserver and cherisher. If we fail to fulfill this role, evil will result for our wives and children. But if we perform our duties as priests in the home, we will mediate divine blessing to our family.

As we said at the outset of this chapter, much of the way in which a man acts as a mediator of divine blessing in his home remains shrouded in difficulty and mystery. What we do know for sure teaches us several crucial lessons.

Lessons

Our conduct as a priest in our home will have a profound spiritual impact on our wife and children.

Men should aspire, therefore, to be a blessing (and not a cursing) to their families by fulfilling their role as a true priest in their home. What is true in the economic realm is true in the spiritual realm to some degree. If we are wise and diligent, this will in general mean that our families will eventually live in comparative prosperity. If we are foolish and lazy, our families will suffer. A man who takes his priestly responsibilities seriously, sets a good example and is spiritually wise and diligent will generally reap a holy and happy wife and family.

Note here the example of Job's family – the birthday celebrations provide witness of how happy his children were and how much they loved each other. There is a connection between the happiness and harmony we see in Job 1:4 and the diligent and wise family priest we see in the next verse. Given what we know about Job's wife, who later urged Job to curse God and die, we can be fairly certain that the happiness of the family was not all the mother's doing.

Ultimately, a happy, harmonious and close-knit family usually requires a father who is a strong spiritual leader. A mother may keep the children under control when they are young, but if Dad is not in charge as they get older, any conflict, disharmony and rebellion will give evidence of the absent male leadership. As men, we dare not abdicate our spiritual leadership to our wives out of fear of conflict, sheer indifference, busyness or any other excuse – we will eventually pay the price, with our folly on display for all to see.

In one sense, there is nothing very mysterious about how we are mediators of divine blessing to our families. The force of our parental example, character and life bring this blessing. If we are weak leaders, passive fathers, or even just "good" men, our general influence for good will diminish. Only godly, assertive leadership will produce a blessed home. We need to cry out for grace, then, to set the spiritual tone of our homes. We must realize that God wants us in control of our homes and families. We should not allow passivity, selfishness or indecision to steal the privilege and blessing of mediating God's grace. We need to take hold of our responsibilities and bless our families by leading them, admonishing them, exhorting them and encouraging them. We must stop being so afraid of saying the wrong thing that we sin by saying nothing at all. If we follow these guidelines, we will keep a clean conscience, set a good example and demand righteousness in our families.

It's too late to abandon responsibility just because we don't want it. The only time for such hesitation was before we got married. We now have the responsibility, and for better or for worse, we will have a profound spiritual impact on our wives, our children and our children's children.

We must verbally communicate divine blessing to our families.

If our verbal communication with our families is predominantly critical and sarcastic, something is drastically wrong. There is a place for criticism in a marriage and family, but it's not a predominant one. We must seek to communicate blessing, positive encouragement and hope for the future to our loved ones. It's easy for us to fall into the habit of critical and negative communication with our families; we often take out our frustrations by blasting the tender souls of our wives and children. This is not how a compassionate priest acts. We should endeavor to bring people back to God, not to drive them away with anger. God didn't ask the priests at high sacrifice every year to curse the people – he asked them to bless the people.

This calls for us to be men of faith. How much our families need our encouragement and blessing! There are times when we are burdened down with responsibilities, worries, concerns and fears, and we need our wives to reassure and encourage us. That said, a man is to be the primary encourager of his wife and family. Our wives need us to encourage them about the future. They need to hear that they are appreciated, that they are doing a good job with the children, that God's promises are true and that by God's grace, the future is still bright with hope. It is our job as priests in our homes to be leaders of faith and courage. If our wives are emotionally weak and tend toward gloom and despair regarding the future, we must not allow this to derail their faith. We must be men of faith ourselves. This kind of faith – determined trust that God's promises are true – is at the heart of what it means to be a man.

In a series of exhortations at the end of 1 Corinthians 16, Paul says in verse 13, "Be on the alert, stand firm in the faith, act like men, be strong." The Greek words for act like men literally meanto act like an adult male. Paul is telling the entire Corinthian church to act with the characteristics of adult males, or men.

Adult men are expected to carry themselves with courage and strength. But where do they find such courage? Paul provides the answer just prior to his command to act like men. "Stand firm in the faith," he writes. Faith enables men to be strong, to be courageous, to be ever alert and ready. It is faith that believes the promises of a God who does not lie and cannot fail. What enables a man to act like a man is that he believes God is true and will keep his promises, no matter what may come.

Men must remember this when troubles and darkness loom over us, making us want to shrink back in fear. We must stand firm in the faith. We must believe God's promises when our wives' grip on them is slipping, when our children cry out for help. It takes faith to be a man of courage and remember that God has promised good to his people. When the bills stack up, when the womb is barren, when an unexpected death comes, when any dark providence assails our family, we must remember that God is true so that with compassion and grace, we can remind our families as well.

This calls for us to communicate vision and encouragement to our children, who are much in need of their father's blessing. Yes, they are sinners who have no hope and are without God in the world. But they are also creatures made in God's image with particular gifts and talents. As fathers, we need to sit down with our children of all ages and paint a picture for them of what a bright future they have if they will follow Christ. We should stress the unique talents God has given them and show them what an awful waste it will be if they squander these gifts on their own lusts and pleasures. We must communicate that they have too much to offer the world and too much to accomplish for the kingdom of God to waste their lives on themselves. If they continue to think only of their own desires, they'll be consigned to a future devoid of hope in this life and the next. But if they turn to God, tremendous blessings will flow to them.

On a related note, fathers need to help their children discern what God has gifted them to do in life. We need to provide direction regarding vocation in light of whom and what God has made our kids to be. We should approach this privilege – and it is indeed a privilege to help mold and shape a life – not with a clumsy, one-size-fits-all approach, but with sensitivity and insight regarding our children's personalities and talents. We are to prepare our kids for life, and one of the main components of that preparation is steering them to a place where they can be blessed and pass blessings on to others. We need to pray for discernment and then exercise the insight God gives us to help our children determine their course in life. By doing so, we'll bless them tremendously.

Application

To any unconverted men who may be reading this book, the best way for you to gain the blessing of God is to respond to his life-changing Gospel.

Don't waste your lives. Don't blow your earthly years on your own selfish desires and miss the enormous blessing God has for everyone who repents and believes in Jesus Christ. You are made in God's image, and so if you repent of your sins, you won't waste your talents on yourself. You can do much for the name of Jesus Christ and the glory of God. When you come to the end of your life, you'll be able to say that you lived in a way that will reverberate for eternity. If that provokes a deep longing in your soul, turn from your sins and believe the promises of God. It's that simple. If you don't believe God's promises, you won't be saved. Not believing his promises tells him that you don't think he can be trusted. If you would be saved and truly bless your family, you must believe the Gospel of Christ – that a holy God became a perfect man to bear our sins and make us righteous before him. Nothing less and nothing more will do. If you act like a true man and humble yourself before God, he will bless you so that you may bless your family.

A wife (or one who hopes to be a wife) should appreciate and understand the enormous burden and responsibility her husband carries.

We will be encouraged if our wives help us and pray earnestly for us. They may (and ought to) rebuke us when necessary, but they shouldn't tear us to pieces with their tongues, thus eroding the foundations of our own happiness and encouragement.

For believing husbands and fathers, this responsibility to bless our families is a heavy burden.

To begin to bear it, we can ask ourselves, "How do we want to be remembered?" When we're losing our temper with our wives or kids, that question just might bring us up short. We can apply the same question to Jesus Christ – how did he want his disciples to remember him? In his last appearance to them, he raised his hands and blessed them. This is our Savior, the one who is the mediator of all the blessings of the New Covenant to every believing man, woman and child. We should remember him that way, then, and not sink under this burden. He will bear us up, hold us, and bless us.

CHAPTER SEVEN

A MAN AS AN INSTRUCTOR
IN SACRED SCRIPTURE

Kids love to role-play. Whether they're shooting each other up as cops and robbers, using their superpowers to save the earth from the forces of evil, or sitting down for a lovely afternoon tea, they dive into their roles with abandon, dressing up in just the right outfits and conjuring up elaborate scenarios they can play out over and over again. It's a timeless part of childhood that helps develop children's imaginations, ambitions and talents. Plus, it's fun to watch.

What our children do in these games for fun, we have been doing very seriously as we discuss men as priests in their homes. We are not merely playing a part by dressing up in priestly costumes and standing among the stage props of a temple. We are putting on the priestly garments that belong to us. We are living in our homes as in a temple and we are doing it for our family's eternal benefit. As we continue to look at this subject, we should not treat it like a kid's dress-up game, but as the sober and joyful truth it really is.

An Instructor in Scripture

The fourth special role of a man as a priest in his home is an instructor in sacred Scripture. One of the clearest emphases of the Old Testament – found in an abundance of passages – is that Israelite priests dispensed instruction regarding God's law. Several passages will show us the importance of the priests' responsibility to instruct the people of God in sacred Scripture. After we see these passages, we'll apply them to a man's role in his home today.

First Samuel 2:12-13 says, "Now the sons of Eli were worthless men; they did not know the LORD and the custom of the priests with the people." The assumption is that Eli's sons were expected to know the customs of the priests so they could properly lead the people. Sadly, they did not possess this knowledge, which was one of their great defects as priests.

Second Kings 12:2 shows the effect of a priest's instruction even on a king. "Jehoash did right in the sight of the LORD all his days in which Jehoiada the priest instructed him."

In 2 Kings 17:27, we read, "Then the king of Assyria commanded, saying, 'Take there one of the priests whom you carried away into exile and let him go and live there; and let him teach them the custom of the god of the land.'" A little background may help. When Assyria carried away the 10 tribes of the northern kingdom into captivity, new settlers took their place in the land of Israel. Because they did not fear God, he sent lions among them which began to kill the people. To quell the attacks, the king of Assyria sent an Israelite priest back to his homeland to inform the new residents how to worship the God of the land. The king assumed the priest knew how to worship God and was therefore responsible to impart that knowledge to the people.

Second Chronicles 15:3 says, "For many days Israel was without the true God and without a teaching priest and without law." This verse is lifted out of a prophecy made by the Spirit of God; it shows that a teaching priest was the great means to bring Israel into contact with the true God and His law. Ezra 7:6, 10, 11 reads:

> This Ezra went up from Babylon, and he was a scribe skilled in the law of Moses, which the LORD God of Israel had given; and the king granted him all he requested because the hand of the LORD his God was upon him ... For Ezra had set his heart to study the law of the LORD and to practice it, and to teach His statutes and ordinances in Israel. Now this is the copy of the decree which King Artaxerxes gave to Ezra the priest, the scribe, learned in the words of the commandments of the LORD and His statutes to Israel.

Verses one to five of this passage describe the genealogy of Ezra, who as a priest in Israel. He had determined to study the law of the Lord and fulfill the priestly tasks of teaching the law's statutes and ordinances in Israel.

In Nehemiah 8:1-9, Ezra carried out his ministry in a manner very similar to what we know as Christian worship. In verse eight, he and the other priests read Scripture aloud, translating as they went so the people would understand the word of God they were hearing. This took place after the Israelite captivity, when the people of God spoke a slightly different dialect as a result of being born in a foreign place.

Jeremiah 2:8 says, "The priests did not say, 'Where is the LORD?' Those who handle the law did not know Me; the shepherds transgressed against Me; the prophets prophesied by Baal and went after things that do not profit." This is a prophecy of condemnation of the priests, who are described as those who handled the law and were responsible for communicating it to the people.

In Jeremiah 18:18, we read, "Then they said, 'Come, let us make plots against Jeremiah, for the law shall not perish from the priest, nor counsel from the wise, nor the word from the prophet. Come, let us strike him with the tongue, and let us not pay attention to any of his words.'" We see here how the word of God affects three different people. It is revelation to the prophet and counsel to the wise man, while the priest's special responsibility is to not let the law of God perish. He is called to hold onto that knowledge and impart it to the people.

All of these passages make plain that one of the chief duties of priests in Israel was to instruct the people in the precepts of the law. There is a great parallel between priests in Israel and a man as a priest in his home who is instructing his family in the Scriptures. This correlation is pointed out explicitly in the pages of the Old Testament, starting in Deuteronomy 4:9-10, which says:

> Only take care, and keep your soul diligently, lest you forget the things that your eyes have seen, and lest they depart from your heart all the days of your life. Make them known to your children and your children's children, how on the day that you stood before the LORD your God at Horeb, the LORD said to me, 'Gather the people to me, that I may let them hear my words, so that they may learn to fear me all the days that they live on the earth, and that they may teach their children so.'

We see the parallel repeated in Deuteronomy 6:4-7, the passage with the famous statement cited by the Lord himself as the first and greatest commandment:

> Hear, O Israel: The LORD our God, the LORD is one. You shall love the LORD your God with all your heart and with all your soul and with all your might. And these words that I command you today shall be on your heart. You shall teach them diligently to your children, and shall talk of them when you sit in your house, and when you walk by the way, and when you lie down, and when you rise.

The same theme surfaces again in Deuteronomy 11:18-19, which says:

> You shall therefore lay up these words of mine in your heart and in your soul, and you shall bind them as a sign on your hand, and they shall be as frontlets between your eyes. You shall teach them to your children, talking of them when you are sitting in your house, and when you are walking by the way, and when you lie down, and when you rise.

These commandments are not regulative only for God's Old Testament people – the call to teach the words of God to our children will never fade away. We are to talk of them at any and every opportunity so that they might fear and love God as soon as is humanly possible.

Application

The passages we've looked at have shown clearly that God has established men as biblical teachers in their homes. If we are to live up to this ideal, how should this principle work out practically in everyday life?

We must know the Scriptures.

Obtaining a knowledge of the Bible requires the two major means God has appointed for spiritual learning: personal Bible study and sitting under the public ministry of the Word. In Deuteronomy 17:18-20, the king in Israel is told to write for himself a copy of the law of God that it might be beside him all the days of his life. He needed to constantly consult God's law – so much so that he had to write it out himself. If the king of God's people put that high of a premium on what God said, how can Christians today do any less? The best means of becoming a good teacher of the word of God is studying it ourselves, as Ezra 7:10 points out, "For Ezra had set his heart to study the Law of the LORD, and to do it and to teach his statutes and rules in Israel." This continues in the New Testament, as the Bereans studied the Scriptures daily to verify the teaching of Paul (Acts 17:11).

If we would instruct our families, we must heed the command of Scripture to engage in consistent personal Bible study. If we are too busy to spend at least a few minutes a day with the Word of God, we are simply too busy. We must take whatever radical steps are necessary to find time to read the Word of God on a daily basis.

But the personal study of the Bible was never intended to be an adequate source of instruction by itself. Sometimes we practice such an individualistic form of Christianity that we convince ourselves we must learn everything we need to know by studying the Bible on our own. We think we're failures if we can't do it. That's far from the truth. We must also set ourselves under a solid public ministry of the Word of God.

Since most of us are not called to study and preach the Bible for our livelihood, the kind of ministry under which we place ourselves is critical. In Ezra 7:10, Ezra not only set himself to study the Word of God, but to teach it in Israel, because such teaching was ordinarily necessary if the Israelite men and women were to come to know the Word of God. In Acts 8:30-35, when Philip asks the Ethiopian eunuch if he understands the Bible he's reading, the eunuch instinctively knows he needs help. "How can I understand," he asks, "except someone guide me?"

Ephesians 4:11-13 teaches that Christ has given needed gifts to the church, including apostles, prophets, evangelists and pastor-teachers, so that the church might come to the fullness of the measure of the stature of Christ. The pastors and ministry we place ourselves under are vitally important if we are to become well-taught priests who can in turn teach our own families. Participating in a local congregation with faithful pastors must be a life priority; as necessary as the homes we live in and the schools our children attend.

We must develop the grace of being spiritually-minded.

According to the biblical texts we've looked at, scriptural instruction should not come exclusively at formal times of family worship. While those times are necessary, we must also teach our families in the natural moments that mark the overflow of a spiritual mind. Such moments are interwoven through all of life, and practicing spiritual-mindedness will help us to bring the Word of God into every situation; whether we're playing with our kids, talking with our wives or sitting at the dinner table.

In today's digital age, the music, television and information overload we face provides constant opportunities to use a biblical worldview to analyze the ethical and practical perspectives that bombard our families. If we watch a television show or listen to a song with our kids, we should be able to spontaneously share a brief biblical viewpoint on what we've just seen or heard. That doesn't have to happen every time, but it should occur often enough that our kids know that God's Word is never far from our minds.

We must plead for the grace to be spiritually-minded. Such grace that will remind us of what the Word of God says about every aspect of our lives. Only this grace, along with fervent prayer and godly discipline, can turn us into the kind of husbands and fathers we ought to be.

We must talk to our families.

It probably seems a little obvious to point this out, but communicating with our families is hard for many men, especially those who tend to nurse a silent, incommunicative reserve. We must avoid schedules and lifestyles that are so busy or selfish that we never take the time to talk to our children about spiritual things. Our kids long especially for attention from their dads. We have to make sure we give it to them through our words.

To help with this, it may work to set up specific times to talk and pray with our wives and individual children regarding spiritual things. One option is to occasionally take each child out to eat alone, and then use some of the time to talk about his or her soul. Perhaps we could block off a portion of Saturday nights or Sunday afternoons to talk with our children. You may choose to speak to one child each week about their understanding of salvation, their spiritual struggles and sins, and any Scripture or catechism questions they may be memorizing. This isn't a legalistic rule. It's good for us to spend time talking to our children. Have we ever asked our children if they are Christians or if they understand and can explain the Gospel? These are simple things, but they're very important to our responsibilities as husbands and fathers. We must talk to our families.

We must commit to stated times in which we teach our families in the Lord.

According to Deuteronomy 6, one of the times we are to talk to our families is when we sit in our houses. This is yet another good argument for family worship, which we discussed in the last chapter. We cannot call ourselves instructors of our families if we never take the time to sit down with them, read a Bible passage and explain how it applies to their lives. To ensure profitable family worship, we may need to spend some of our own devotional time briefly planning how we're going to approach it and what we want to say. This is a common practice of godly men that we should emulate.

We must support the instruction our family receives through the church we attend.

The teaching and preaching of pastors in the local church is an extension of our own priestly instruction in our homes. We need to make sure we do not set our children up to think lightly of the church by criticizing their pastors or teachers in front of them. Rather, we should praise and speak well of these leaders. We can't expect our children to look up to their pastors or follow their teaching if we're always badmouthing them. May God grant that our children's heroes will not be rock stars or athletes, but pastors and men of God

CHAPTER EIGHT
A MAN AS A JUDGE IN HOLY THINGS

We come now to the fifth and final role of a priest which a man in his home must fulfill. The role of a judge in holy things is closely related to being an instructor in sacred Scripture. Yet, it's important enough to consider on its own.

A judge is not just a legal scholar or an instructor in a law school, although he may serve both of those functions. He is something more. A judge is required to apply the law to specific cases, render a verdict in those cases and then deal out appropriate punishment or implement needed change. A judge is very practical. He makes decisions that affect people's lives. So it is in our homes. Our judgment is what stands. Even though we may struggle and make less than perfect decisions, God has appointed us as judges. Our families (even our teenagers) are called to submit to our leadership.

Here, we can begin to see the difference in the roles of instructor and judge. If men possess a common failing in spiritual things, it is getting carried away with complex, theoretical and abstract doctrine while being unable to apply all they know in a practical way. They may have a doctorate in theology, but often find trouble in ruling their homes well or in making the simplest ethical decision wisely. Solomon says of such men in Proverbs 17:24, "Wisdom is in the presence of the one who has understanding, but the eyes of a fool are on the ends of the earth." The fool is impractical. He focuses on what is out of reach rather than what is right in front of him. Foolish men, for example, will endlessly discuss different theories with regard to the imputation of Adam's sin while their children wreck the house and drive their mother to pull her hair out. This common failing of men makes it crucial to emphasize that as priests in our homes. We must fill the judge's role by practically applying our scriptural knowledge in real life situations each day.

As we've done previously, we'll see in this chapter how priests fulfilled the role of judge in Israel. Then, we look at what the Bible says about how we can serve the same role in our own homes. We'll close the chapter out with several practical applications.

Israelite Priests as Judges

The priests of Israel were called to serve as the judges or adjudicators of questions related to holy things. This role first emerges clearly in Leviticus 13 and 14, where the priest makes all the judgment calls regarding leprosy. Was a certain case leprosy or was it not? It was the priest's decision. When a case of leprosy was confirmed, should the whole house be torn down? Should the person be sent out of the city? The priest made these judgments, as well as any other needed decisions about what was going to happen.

This same role is evident in Leviticus 27, where the priest was to make practical judgments about the value of certain items owed to the Lord. If an Israelite made a vow, but couldn't pay exactly what he had offered to the Lord, his promise had to be evaluated. Who made the evaluation? According to the text, "The priest shall value him...the priest shall value it as good or bad...the priest shall calculate the price." In Numbers 5, the priest is the one who administers and applies the test for adultery to the woman whose husband is suspicious of her. When Israel finally conquered Canaan, it was Eleazar the priest, along with Joshua, who apportioned the inheritances in the land to the various tribes.

Deuteronomy 17:9, 12 says:

> So you shall come to the Levitical priest or the judge who is in office in those days, and you shall inquire of them and they will declare to you the verdict in the case...The man who acts presumptuously by not listening to the priest who stands there to serve the LORD your God, nor to the judge, that man shall die; thus you shall purge the evil from Israel.

The priests were not lecturing on the principles of God's law in this passage. In these cases, the priests were there to give a verdict in a case, and the people were then bound to abide by the decision.

In Ezra 10:10-11, we read:

> Then Ezra the priest stood up and said to them, 'You have been unfaithful and have married foreign wives adding to the guilt of Israel. Now therefore, make confession to the LORD God of your fathers and do His will; and separate yourselves from the peoples of the land and from the foreign wives.'

In this instance, Ezra is rendering his verdict in the case of Israelites marrying foreign wives. This is how a priest fulfilled the role of judge. He gave the verdict (here, the offending party was guilty as charged), and then handed out the punishment for the crime.

Haggai 2:11 commands the people: "Thus says the LORD of hosts, 'Ask now the priests for a ruling.'" The point is that it was the priest who made this application of law. It wasn't just anyone in the land of Israel.

In each of these key passages, it is clear that in any specific case where there was a question about the application and implementation of the law of God, the priest was the ultimate authority. It was not his duty merely to instruct the people in the law. Rather, he had to decide how the law specifically applied and then enforce the law's observance with penalties.

A Man as a Judge in His Home

Wives

This picture of an Old Testament priest finds an exact parallel in a man who is a priest in his home. First Peter 3:6-7 instructs us on how we should relate to our wives:

> Just as Sarah obeyed Abraham, calling him lord, and you have become her children if you do what is right without being frightened by any fear. You husbands in the same way, live with

your wives in an understanding way, as with someone weaker, since she is a woman; and show her honor as a fellow heir of the grace of life, so that your prayers will not be hindered.

The text plainly teaches that wives are to obey their husbands in practical matters, regarding their husbands as exercising lordship over them. This implies the right and duty of the husband to act as a judge in practical, ethical matters relating to his wife.

Children

With reference to children, Paul says in Ephesians 6:4, "Fathers, do not provoke your children to anger, but bring them up in the discipline and instruction of the Lord." On the face of it, this text proves that men should be instructors of their families. A closer look reveals that we should also act as judges.

The idea of instruction is present in both of the words used in this text. It could read, "bring them up in the instruction and instruction of the Lord." In fact, these Greek words are both translated as instruction in other places in the Bible. The standard Greek-English lexicon gives the same meaning (*instruction*) for both words. What is interesting is the specific flavor of both forms of instruction mentioned in the verse. The first word, discipline, refers literally to the training of children. The lexicon also suggests various other translations, including upbringing, training, discipline and correction. Such action involves much more than abstract instruction. Fathers are to act not only as teachers, but as judges who correct and punish their children, thus training them in the Lord.

The second word, though it is translated instruction, also has two other translations suggested in the lexicon: *admonition* and warning. This is in fact, the common root meaning of to *admonish* in the New Testament. This particular word is used in two other places in the New Testament. Titus 3:10 instructs Titus to "Reject a factious man after a first and second warning." After Paul recounts the horrific judgments that overtook Israel because of its sin in the wilderness, he says in 1 Corinthians 10:11, "Now these things happened to them as an example, and they were written for our instruction …" Paul is referring to Israel's immorality and the subsequent punishment for its sins. These events were written for our warning, admonition, and instruction.

In Ephesians 6:4, both usages of the word *instruction* go beyond mere information to imply instruction communicated in the form of warning. A father is obligated to warn his children. He should say such things as, "Son, you need to stay away from that crowd at school – they will only lead you down the wrong path." Or, he may say, "Honey, I'm sorry, but you may not watch that movie. It has no redeeming value."

As priests in our homes, we cannot afford to be arm-chair, Monday-morning quarterbacks, observing from a distance and second-guessing after the fact. We must be involved, and our instruction must apply to specific cases and be enforced by verbal warnings and appropriate penalties. In short, we must not only be a legal (biblical) scholar, but we must function as a judge as well.

Application

Our duty to be a judge does not negate our need for wisdom and counsel.

We should not act like arrogant jerks just because we are the judge and we have authority. We should seek our wife's counsel, and in difficult situations, ask for our pastor's advice. Our duty to be a judge doesn't automatically bestow all power and all knowledge upon us. We still need advice from others. Then, when all is said and done, we must do what we believe biblical wisdom demands. We must be firm, but careful to infuse our authority with humility and grace towards our families.

Our duty to judge does not mean that we must become overly strict so that we always err on the side of severity.

When some men realize they are called to implement the law of God in their family, they think that means they've got to become a hanging judge. Fortunately, that's not the case. Occupying a judgeship does not mean that we should always err on the safe side by inflicting punishments that are too severe. If we err on the side of severity, we simply get it wrong. If we err on the side of indulgence, we simply get it wrong there also. We must judge righteously, without veering into the ditch on the right or the canyon on the left. But we're not alone, nor left to our own resources. Grace and humility before God will allow us to walk this tenuous tightrope.

Our duty to be a judge rebukes our selfish desire to be left alone.

Our natural male inclination doesn't want to deal with the everyday problems requiring decisions from us. We want to wimp out behind the newspaper or in front of the television. But, a judge has to judge, and there will often be a backload of cases when we walk through the door at night. We cannot be absentee landlords. We must realize that it is our responsibility to give practical application and implementation to the principles of God's Holy Word in our homes.

We cannot delegate this responsibility to our wives, although we should often seek their counsel and weigh carefully what they say. In the end, we must do what we believe is right before God. It is nobody's responsibility but our own to be a judge in our home. If we expect the moral and ethical decisions we make to truly promote godliness and holiness, they must come with the full and decisive weight of our moral headship as the judge of our home.

We must follow through on our teaching with practical application and enforcement.

We must imitate Calvin and not Luther, as Warfield describes in his book, *Calvin and Calvinism*:

> When Calvin came to Geneva, he tells us himself, he found the gospel preached there, but no church established … He would have found much the same state of things everywhere else in the Protestant world … As a recent historian – Professor Karl Rieker – rather flippantly expresses it: "Luther, when he had preached and

sowed the seed of the Word, left to the Holy Spirit the care of producing the fruit, while with his friend Philip he peacefully drank his glass of Wittenberg beer." Calvin could not take this view of the matter. "Whatever others may hold," he observed, "we cannot think so narrowly of our office that when preaching is done our task is fulfilled, and we may take our rest." In his view the mark of a true Church is not merely that the gospel is preached in it, but that it is "followed."[1]

The mark of a Christian home is not merely that the Gospel is preached in it, but that the Gospel is lived there. It is our job as priests to make sure that happens. Here is where the real work is, and where we most often fail. Yet unless we carry through on our instruction and doctrine, our wives and children will suffer greatly.

We must seek to create in our homes a climate of holiness and ethical righteousness.

This was the whole point of the priests' function as adjudicators in Israel. Their goal was to maintain in Israel the motto, "Holiness to the Lord." To follow in that tradition, we should apply Psalm 101:6-8 to ourselves:

> My eyes shall be upon the faithful of the land, that they may dwell with me; He who walks in a blameless way is the one who will minister to me. He who practices deceit shall not dwell within my house; he who speaks falsehood shall not maintain his position before me. Every morning I will destroy all the wicked of the land, so as to cut off from the city of the LORD all those who do iniquity.

These verses describe how the king of Israel is going to drive the wicked out of the land and maintain purity in the nation. As the king of our homes, we should adhere to the same principle. We must be committed *every morning* to rooting out sin and driving out wickedness in order to maintain an atmosphere of holiness. Proverbs

---

[1] Benjamin B. Warfield, *Calvin and Calvinism*, vol. 5 of *The Works of Benjamin B. Warfield* (Grand Rapids: Baker Book House, 1981), 15-16.

26:20 says, "The wise king winnows the wicked and drives the threshing wheel over them." We probably shouldn't drive a threshing wheel over our wives and children, but we must deal aggressively with any sin that disrupts the climate of peace and purity we are striving to create.

One of the major areas we'll have to make practical judgments in is the consumption of television, movies and music by our families. In era of instantaneous Internet access, cell phones with text messaging, digital music players and hundreds of channels, we must keep a close eye on what our children are reading, listening to and watching. We must be ready to point out – and forbid – anything that is contrary to the Word of God and that drives our children further from righteousness.

We will also need to keep watch over the relationships between our children to ensure they maintain a healthy interaction among one another. An older son shouldn't continually provoke his younger siblings so they grow up to hate him. Younger brothers or sisters shouldn't aggravate and tattle. In any situation, we must determine to the best of our ability who is right and who is wrong, discipline the sinning child and teach him to act correctly towards his siblings. When he asks forgiveness, they should grant it; we should model this process to make sure it occurs over and over in our homes. We must also teach our children to treat their parents respectfully, including the occasional and appropriate use of "Yes, Sir" and "Yes, Ma'am."

We should expect more than merely surface behavior in our families. We must look for a truly sweet spirit in our wives and children. Our kids shouldn't snarl when they get out of bed in the morning. They shouldn't talk back to their mother and they shouldn't grumble over every little request. We must confront their sins – even seemingly minor ones – and show them how Christ would have them live. We must also repent of anything we have done to offend our families. If we don't admit our faults and ask for forgiveness, our moral authority will be compromised.

By way of encouragement, we have the right and privilege to be the judge of our homes.

God has granted us the moral authority to make the final decision about what will be right and wrong in our homes. As clear as this may be in Scripture, it can be difficult for some men to get hold of practically. The situations in which we have to make these kinds of judgments are often packed with emotion, such as when a son is mad at his mother, or when teenagers are at each other's throats. It's not easy to make a judgment when we know someone is going to be unhappy no matter what we say. But, we have the right – indeed, the obligation – to do so. God has appointed men to lead their families, and so we must.

The task often seems even more difficult because we are not infinite in wisdom. It's easy to draw the ethical line too tightly or too broadly. Often, we will see consequences and fallout from our decisions. We may make our children angry. Our wives may not be happy with us. Our judgments may seem narrow or loose to our friends. Given the cultural atmosphere where we are constantly told to tolerate whatever our kids do, we have a tough job. But, we're called to do what we know is right in a given situation.

Because of all this, we should be encouraged that we have the right to be judges of the ethical standards in our own homes. As Christians, we should remember that God will be with us as we make judgments. He will give wisdom and bless our decisions as we make them in good conscience before him. He may not bless us if we are arrogant jerks who don't seek counsel and refuse to listen to our wives' opinions. He also may not bless us if we reject the moral standards of his Word. But if we make a prayerful, godly, humble, good-faith effort to maintain an atmosphere of biblical holiness and purity in our homes, God will overrule our marginal mistakes, honor our feeble efforts and increase our small stock of wisdom and courage. If God calls men to be the judge of their homes – and he does – then he will be with us as we carry out that duty.

These principles clearly underscore our need of constant divine grace.

These duties expose our lack of practical wisdom in nitty-gritty matters. They lay bare our lack of patience in gathering the necessary information to make a wise decision. They bring to light our moral inconsistency when we must make ethical decisions that will demand changes in our own actions. An agonizing sense of inadequacy should not make us give up or run away, but should drive us over and over to the blood and blessing of the everlasting covenant (Hebrews 13:20-21). God has given us an enormous burden with these responsibilities. On our own, we will fail. But, his unfailing mercy has not left us alone. If we fall to our knees before the throne of grace, we will "receive mercy and may find grace to help in time of need" (Hebrews 4:16). What more could we ask for than a promise such as this, backed by the maker of heaven and earth? We shall not fail; we must not fail. God giving us strength, will not fail.

CHAPTER NINE
SPIRITUAL QUALIFICATIONS OF A MAN AS PRIEST IN HIS HOME

In our study of the special roles of a man as a priest in his home, we have looked primarily at outward appearance and conduct as we fulfill our God-given duties. In this chapter, however, we will look more closely at the heart, spirit and character. Our priesthood in our homes depends not primarily on what we do, but on who we are.

As we study examples of priests in the Bible, three premiere characteristics of priesthood stand out. The Bible presents these traits, which only the Spirit of God can produce, as essential character qualities for a true priest. As faith, hope, and love are the three great marks of true Christianity, so these three qualities – blamelessness, compassion, and faithfulness – are the chief marks of a true godly priest. We'll look at each of these characteristics in turn.

What is Blamelessness?

Every genuine priest in the Word of God was required to be blameless. We've already looked at a prime example of this. Job 1:1 says, "There was a man in the land of Uz whose name was Job; and that man was blameless, upright, fearing God and turning away from evil." The fourfold description of Job's integrity in this verse begins (and is summed up by) the first characteristic. Job was *blameless*, as the NASB translates it. The KJV translates the word *perfect*. Job was blameless or perfect in the sense of being morally complete. He was not sinless, but no particular sin so manifested itself as to form a blot, blemish or deficiency in his general character.

The Greek version of the Old Testament translates the word *blameless* or *complete*. The derivation of this word literally means *without blame*. This same word is used in Luke 1:5-6, which says:

> In the days of Herod, king of Judea, there was a priest named Zacharias, of the division of Abijah; and he had a wife from the daughters of Aaron, and her name was Elizabeth. They were both righteous in the sight of God, walking *blamelessly* in all the commandments and requirements of the Lord.

The description is actually applied to both Zacharias and his wife Elizabeth, reinforcing the idea that if a man is to be blameless, it is vitally important that his wife also be blameless. Though the NASB translation does not reflect it, the word blameless is placed at the very end of the description of Zacharias' character, just as it came at the beginning of the description of Job's character. We might translate the verse, "They were both righteous in the sight of God, walking in all the commandments and requirements of the Lord – blameless." Thus the word blameless – without obvious moral defect in his reputation – sums up Zacharias' character before men.

Under the Old Covenant, priests were required to be physically blameless – a foreshadowing of the spiritual blamelessness required of priests in the New Covenant. Leviticus 21:21-23 says:

> No man among the descendants of Aaron the priest who has a defect is to come near to offer the LORD'S offerings by fire; since he has a defect, he shall not come near to offer the food of his God…only he shall not go in to the veil or come near the altar because he has a defect, so that he will not profane My sanctuaries. For I am the LORD who sanctifies them.

Just as the priests of the Old Testament were to be without obvious physical defect, so we are to be without evident spiritual defect as priests in our homes.

Lessons from Blamelessness

This blameless character of true priests suggests several lessons for men.

First, being a blameless priest in our homes is a realistic and attainable goal.

This is not some sort of hypothetical ideal set before us that no human being has ever lived up to. We know from the word of God that at least two men actually were blameless. God doesn't show us these examples only to convince us of how sinful we are. This is something that Job *was*. This is something that Zacharias *was*. Because these men could be blameless, we are not allowed to shift this responsibility off. We're actually supposed to *be* blameless by the grace of our Lord Jesus Christ.

We live in a time where the morally defective character and the remaining depravity of Christians have been over-emphasized. The doctrines of easy-believism, carnal Christianity and cheap grace have led to a host of professing Christians whose lives are terribly inconsistent and blatantly defective. To speak of living a blameless life to these kinds of people seems almost a denial of the grace of God. But, the example of Job and Zacharias teaches us plainly that a blameless life is a realistic and attainable goal. A true Christian's character can and should be without moral deficiency before the eyes of his family and his fellow man.

Second, being a blameless priest in our homes is a necessary and crucial goal.

Blamelessness is a foundation for everything else. If we are not blameless, we will undermine every one of our special roles as a priest in our homes. If we are morally defective, we won't be able to intercede for our families. Psalm 66:18-19 says, "If I regard wickedness in my heart, the Lord will not hear; But certainly God has heard; He has given heed to the voice of my prayer." The text does not say, "If I *have* wickedness in my heart, the Lord will not hear," because each one of us has iniquity in his heart. It says, "If I *regard* wickedness in my heart, the Lord will not hear." Some of us may be regarding iniquity, or harboring a darling sin without repentance. Doing so will subvert our ability to pray for our families.

It will also weaken our role as a mediator of divine blessing. Such blessing depends on the fact that the head of the household is righteous. If we are righteous, our house may be described as the house of the righteous. If we are wicked, how can God's blessings descend on our homes?

Further, a lack of blamelessness will undercut our roles as a director of religious worship and an instructor in sacred Scripture. We will lack moral authority in the eyes of our families if we have anything less than a blameless walk. Our wives and children are keenly aware of any inconsistency in our lives. If we indulge ourselves in anything out of step with our established convictions about the Scriptures, our actions will open us up to the charge of hypocrisy and tempt our wives and children to cynicism.

In addition, we will damage our role as a judge in holy things if we are not blameless. When we constantly have to justify ourselves in a path of sin, we cannot maintain the fine discernment and moral sensitivity necessary to the role. Not dealing with sin clouds our consciences, makes our character defective and corrupts our whole being. Such negligence often causes us to react too harshly or too easily to what happens in our homes.

Third, living as a blameless priest in our homes demands open and honest dealing with our sins, not perfection.

It demands, in other words, that we live by the Gospel of Christ. To be a blameless priest, we don't have to keep the law perfectly. But, we must live by the Gospel consistently, especially in regard to whatever specific sins may be derailing our ministry and influence in our homes.

Christians will sin and even blameless priests will sin. Sinfulness is in our very nature and will never be completely eradicated until we reach glory. But here's the great thing about being a Christian – all of us get to repent. Pastors get to repent. Men get to repent. Women get to repent. Children get to repent. The standard for being a Christian is not perfection. It is His atoning sacrifice that allows us to repent of our sins each day.

It is important that we not sin. But, it is equally important – and perhaps even more so – that we repent. It is one thing for us to lose our temper, watch a questionable television program with our family, be careless in ordering family worship, fail to discipline our children or make a selfish decision about our time, and then, realizing our sin, to openly repent and ask forgiveness. It is a completely different thing – and vastly worse – to commit the same sins and justify ourselves or be hardened in our sin rather than repent. David committed adultery and repented. If we commit adultery and don't repent, we are headed for a very different fate than David.

First John 2:1-2 says, "My little children, I am writing these things to you so that you may not sin. But if anyone does sin, we have an advocate with the Father, Jesus Christ the righteous. He is the propitiation for our sins, and not for ours only, but also for the sins of the whole world." If we are justifying ourselves in a course of sin or if there is a moral defect that we refuse to deal with, we need to repent. The Gospel gives us the opportunity to do so. The grace of God is this: that we can turn back to him and be blameless once again. But we can't go on refusing to deal with our sin. Repentance is the only way for us to reclaim our moral authority and leadership in the home. Nothing else we may do can repair the influence of our defective and hypocritical character. The longer we go on in hardness of heart, the more damage we are doing to our home spiritually.

Both Job and Zacharias sinned. In the succeeding verses in Luke 1, we see that Zacharias erred so grievously that God struck him dumb for nine months. Job also sinned as he struggled to understand the providence of God that seemed so set against him. But both of these priests repented, turned from evil and continued to be blameless. The difference in Christians and non-Christians is not that one sins and the other doesn't. It's that Christians repent when they sin. Thus, part of our role as a blameless priest before our families is humble confession of sin to them. How can we know if we're a blameless priest to our family? If we've never repented in front of them, we're most likely not blameless. One of the marks of a true Christian is that he goes on confessing his sins and Christ goes on forgiving his sins and cleansing him from all unrighteousness. One of the marks of a true priest is that he goes on confessing his sins before his family, and they go on forgiving him. Such confession will not erode a family's respect for a man and his authority. Rather, it's the only thing that will get it back. As long as we continue to piously throw around our weight in the home without such plain dealings before our families, they will continue to think of us as, at best, pompous, proud windbags.

Once we have made a clean confession of our sins, we must back it up with fruits fitting for repentance. We must exhibit, in the language of the catechism, "new endeavors after true obedience." We won't perfectly fulfill the ideal of obedience, but we should make new efforts toward that end. Our families don't have to see us acting perfectly. But, they do have to see us trying to deal with sin, whether it be a bad temper, selfishness, neglect of our families or any of a hundred other things. Only true repentance will enable us to be blameless priests in our homes.

Fourth, living as a blameless priest in our home should point us to the Lord Jesus Christ as the prime example and source of the grace we need to be blameless.

Hebrews 7:26 makes plain that our Lord is the highest example of a blameless priest: "For it was fitting for us to have such a high priest, holy, innocent, undefiled, separated from sinners and exalted above the heavens." It would be wrong of us to think about blameless priests and not lift our eyes to Christ. Our goal should be to live as He lived. As 1 John 2:6 says, "The one who says he abides in him ought himself to walk in the same manner as he walked." Christ Himself is the source of the blamelessness that we need.

What is Compassion?

Compassion is a tender concern and loving sympathy born of difficult personal experiences. It's the empathetic love we feel for someone who is enduring suffering or difficulties that we have also experienced. A cancer survivor is more likely to understand the feelings of someone who has just been diagnosed with the disease than someone who has never been afflicted with cancer. Compassion means that we feel from the inside what that other person feels. When we have suffered (or can easily imagine suffering) in the same way they have, it gives an extra dimension to the love we show them.

The example of Job is again relevant to how a true priest should live with compassion. When Job said of his children, "Perhaps my sons have sinned and cursed God in their hearts," he was speaking as a man experienced in the evil of the human heart, the temptations of the world, and the peculiar struggles of youth. He well knew how even the legitimate feasting of a birthday celebration could become the occasion for grievous sin in his children. That was his personal experience. But flowing out of this experience was his tender concern for his children. He did not say, "If they have cursed God in their hearts, I will never speak to them again." Neither did he say, "If they have cursed God in their hearts, well, that's just the way kids are, they'll grow out of it." His compassionate concern was for their welfare, and that concern manifested itself in actions intended to restore wayward children to divine favor.

Every true priest ideally ought to exhibit the same quality. Hebrews 5:2 says, "He [the high priest] can deal gently with the ignorant and misguided, since he himself also is beset with weakness." As we saw in the first chapter, the word translated *gently* by the NASB conveys the idea that a priest is to always act with measured feeling. He is to restrain his indignation, anger, and impatience that naturally rise when he sees the sin, ignorance, and moral follies of men. Only true compassion will enable him to act as a priest with moderation and gentleness.

Lessons from Compassion

The compassionate character of a true priest suggests several lessons for us as men.

First, we must take sin seriously.

We need to have a deep sense of the awful consequences sin brings in its wake. We must be committed to stopping its course in those whom we love and minister to–our wives and children. A priest's life work is to deal with the consequences of sin by restoring sinners to God and delivering them from the calamities sin will bring upon them. If, then, we are to be priests in our homes, we must maintain a tender conscience and a vigorous commitment to deal with sin in ourselves and in our family.

Second, we must maintain a delicate balance between indulgence and severity.

This is a hard thing to do. The attitude which tolerates and even condones transgressions of the law of God in our wives or children is often rooted in a self-indulgent view of the sins of our youth. On the other hand, the severity which angrily over-reacts to the mistakes of immature and ignorant young people is often the result of self-righteousness which has conveniently forgotten the enormous amount of youthful iniquity for which God has forgiven us. As priests, we should remember our own weaknesses so that we find the appropriate balance of compassion and principle in dealing with the sins of our family members.

Third, we should always deal with the sins of our family members with an eye to their restoration to divine favor and blessing.

In every discipline situation, in every confrontation and decision, one of the decisive factors in how we deal with the situation should be the best spiritual interest of the sinner. Our response should come with metered emotion. We don't want to err by merely placing a Band-Aid on the wound that sin has made, saying, "peace, peace," when there is no peace. On the other hand, we don't want to drive the sinner to such despair that he hopelessly abandons himself to sin. We should always be thinking, "How can I best deal with this person so as to bring them back to God?" We must take both sin and the sinner's need seriously.

Fourth, we must look to the Lord Jesus Christ as the great example and source of such compassion (Hebrews 2:17-18; 4:14-16).

The guidance and strength we need to exercise such a priesthood, will come only as we look unto Jesus, the author and perfecter of our faith.

What is Faithfulness?

Again, we look first to Job. The last words of Job 1:5 say, "Thus Job did *continually*." Literally, the text means *all the days*. The emphasis is on Job's consistency as a priest in his home. He was reliable and trustworthy. His family could count on him. Every time the appointed hour for the family sacrifice came, Job was there doing his job. We're meant to infer that in all of Job's other responsibilities as a priest in his home, he was also faithful.

This quality of faithfulness in a true priest is underscored in similar language elsewhere in the Old Testament. In 1 Samuel 2:35, God says, "But I will raise up for Myself a faithful priest who will do according to what is in My heart and in My soul; and I will build him an enduring house, and he will walk before My anointed always." God says that in contrast to the unfaithfulness of Eli and his sons, He would raise up a faithful priest for Himself. It is interesting that verse 35 ends with the same words as Job 1:5–this priest will walk before God's anointed *all the days*. The phrase underscores the priest's faithfulness. Like Job, he was going to be regular, constant, and consistent in his ministry.

Yet, the key idea here lies in the adjective *faithful*. The man God was planning to raise up was to be a faithful priest. The root word used is very common in Hebrew and means to be firm, solid, true, or enduring. It is also used in the phrase *an enduring house* in the same verse. An enduring house is one that remains. In other passages, the same root word refers to belief in God. We believe in things because they are true. In the 1 Samuel verse, the word carries the idea of someone who is trustworthy and reliable, or faithful. A faithful priest is one who continues in his responsibilities all the days. This faithfulness has two aspects. It includes faithfulness to the Lord. God says the faithful priest "will do according to what is in My heart and in My soul" (1 Samuel 2:35). This is in stark contrast to the sons of Eli, who according to 1 Samuel 2:12, "did not know the Lord and the custom of the priests with the people."

The second aspect relates to the people of God. As we saw previously, the vital role of the priestly office is to restore sinners to the Lord. Eli's sons abused the worshippers at Shiloh by taking raw meat that they did not deserve. They also seemed to think it appropriate to lie with the women who served at the doorway of the tent of meeting. On the other hand, Samuel had no such faults in his character. Given the chance to respond, even the people of Israel agreed that he had been faithful to them (1 Samuel 12:1-5; cf. Luke 12:41-48). To emulate Samuel (as opposed to the sons of Eli) means that as priests, we should fight the worldly lusts which would cause us to take advantage of the very ones to whom we should be ministering. We should perform our role in a careful, trustworthy, reliable manner.

Lessons from Faithfulness

There are sobering lessons in this for us.

First, as priests in our homes, we should display persevering consistency (or faithfulness) in our duties.

Our wives and children should be able to count on us to hold regular family worship, to manifest consistent principles in dealing with family issues, to be unswerving in leading them to church and caring for their souls.

Second, we should remember that our main concern is our family's spiritual welfare.

Thus, we should discipline ourselves for that ministry. We should not treat our families as mere vehicles to fulfill our fleshly desires for pleasure and ease. It is so easy for us to become self-centered. When we find ourselves slipping into that mode, we need to remember that if we take care of God's business, he will take care of our needs and desires. We shouldn't think of our wives as created merely to satisfy our needs and desires for sexual fulfillment. We shouldn't use our children to fulfill our own frustrated desires for success or reputation. Our main concern should be their spiritual well-being. If we do what is best for our families by placing their needs before our own, we will find plenty of legitimate satisfaction in them.

Finally, as priests in our home, we behold in our own high priest the great example and source of faithful, priestly ministry.

No one ever ministered more faithfully than the Lord Jesus Christ. A true Christian man knows that in his head (from reading the Scriptures) and also in his heart (from the Lord's faithfulness in his own life).

CHAPTER TEN

HOPE FOR A MAN AS A PRIEST
IN HIS HOME

A man who wants to live as a godly, caring leader in a world that mocks such principles may feel overwhelmed at the thought of living up to the biblical standard of a husband and father. He may look at the vast amounts of work that go into living as a godly priest and be discouraged with the thought of how many times he has failed. Such men should take heart! There is hope to be found in Christ's embodiment of the qualities and characteristics of a true priest.

Jesus Christ is the great and true priest because he offered the one and only sacrifice for sin. He now sits at God's right hand, ready to save all that come unto God by Him. A sinner in desperate trouble can find in Christ all the qualities he could ever need. Christ is a blameless priest. Even cynics and skeptics who see the worst in everyone will never find a defect in Him. God Himself found no blemish in His Son or in His Son's sacrifice.

Christ is also a compassionate priest. He doesn't allow His just anger for our sins to break the restraining chains of His patience and love. But He also doesn't treat our sins and failures with superficial sentiment. Christ deals with our sins in a firm but gentle manner, always showing that He loves us.

Further, Christ is a faithful priest. He will never fail to serve as our priest. He will always be praying and interceding for His children. Even when we think we can't pray for ourselves, He will be faithful to us. We have now – and we will always have – Jesus Christ as our great high priest and advocate with the Father.

The wonderful thing is that there is no need for anyone to feel that he is beyond the reach of God's grace. No matter who a man is, what he has done, or how guilty he feels, Jesus Christ is ready to be a blameless, compassionate and faithful high priest to him. We learn about the office of priest in the Bible because God is in the business of bringing men back to Himself even as He deals with their sin. He does this through the one true and final priest, the Savior of sinners with whom every man needs a personal relationship. This is what Christianity means–to need and to know and to have a blameless, compassionate, and faithful priest before God.

No human who has ever lived can do without that blameless priest to stand in his place and give him title to the blessings of God. We can't gain these blessings on our own. Sin makes us so low, weak, and depraved that we end up flat on our backs, in desperate need of compassion and grace. We are like a blind man walking on the edge of a cliff. We don't realize how merciful God has been to us already and how much we need someone – a faithful priest – to take us by the hand and lead us to safety. When we cry out to God for mercy, God will answer our prayers and send us Christ as a compassionate priest to keep us from falling off the cliff. He exchanges His righteousness for our sin and we're adopted into the family of God. Only then can we truly begin to live as a priest in our home.

While we serve as a priest, we often wonder how God can keep forgiving us for our mistakes. But if He commanded His disciples to forgive their brethren seven times a day, and seventy times seven, He will certainly do the same Himself. We worry whether or not He will preserve us when we face a new situation. But, we must remember that we have a faithful priest who will bear with us all the days.

How will we ever become the kind of man God wants us to be? Again and again, when our sins are set before us, and we feel our weakness, our lack of compassion, our inconsistency and defectiveness, those issues should drive us back to Jesus Christ. He is the one who says, "He who believes in Me, as the Scripture said, 'From his innermost being will flow rivers of living water.'" He is the one who, as Paul says, will transform us from glory to glory when we behold Him (2 Corinthians 3:18).

That transformation takes place when we live in the presence of Jesus Christ. Like Moses, who dwelt in the presence of God's glory on the mountain, our faces will shine with His glory. We have to live with Christ. We've got to wake up with Him. We've got to walk with Him. We've got to end the day with Him. We have to be with Him always. We have to read His Word and speak to Him. As we do, the glory of what Christ is as a priest will begin to enlighten us as well. May God grant it to be so for each one of us.

CPSIA information can be obtained
at www.ICGtesting.com
Printed in the USA
BVHW030754141022
649115BV00009B/122